LIGHTING DESIGN

By reading this book, you will develop the skills to perceive a space and its contents *in light*, and be able to devise a layout of luminaires that will provide that lit appearance.

Written by renowned lighting expert Christopher (Kit) Cuttle, the book:

- explains the difference between vision and perception, which is the distinction between providing lighting to make things visible, and providing it to influence the appearance of everything that is visible;
- demonstrates how lighting patterns generated by three-dimensional objects interacting with directional lighting are strongly influential upon how the visual perception process enables us to recognise object attributes, such as lightness, colourfulness, texture and gloss;
- reveals how a designer who understands the role of these lighting patterns in the perceptual process may employ them either to reveal, or to subdue, or to enhance the appearance of selected object attributes by creating appropriate spatial distributions of light;
- carefully explains calculational techniques and provides easy-to-use spreadsheets, so that layouts of lamps and luminaires are derived that can be relied upon to achieve the required illumination distributions.

Practical lighting design involves devising three-dimensional light fields that create luminous hierarchies related to the visual significance of each element within a scene. By providing you with everything you need to develop a design concept – from the understanding of how lighting influences human perceptions of surroundings, through to engineering efficient and effective lighting solutions – Kit Cuttle instils in his readers a new-found confidence in lighting design.

Christopher 'Kit' Cuttle, MA, FCIBSE, FIESANZ, FIESNA, FSLL, is visiting lecturer in Advanced Lighting Design at the Queensland University of Technology, Brisbane, Australia, and is author of two books on lighting (*Lighting by Design, 2nd edition, Architectural Press*, 2008; and *Light for Art's Sake, Butterworth Heinemann, 2007)*. His previous positions include Head of Graduate Education in Lighting at the Lighting Research Center, Rensselaer Polytechnic Institute, Troy, New York; Senior Lecturer at the Schools of Architecture at the University of Auckland and the Victoria University of Wellington, both in New Zealand; Section Leader in the Daylight Advisory Service, Pilkington Glass; and Lighting Designer with Derek Phillips Associates, both in the UK. His recent awards include the Society of Light and Lighting's Leon Gaster 2013 Award for his LR&T paper 'A New Direction for General Lighting Practice', and the Lifetime Achievement Award presented at the 2013 Professional Lighting Design Conference in Copenhagen.

LIGHTING DESIGN

A perception-based approach

Christopher Cuttle

Routledge
Taylor & Francis Group

LONDON AND NEW YORK

First published 2015
by Routledge
2 Park Square, Milton Park, Abingdon, Oxon OX14 4RN

and by Routledge
711 Third Avenue, New York, NY 10017

Routledge is an imprint of the Taylor & Francis Group, an informa business

British Library Cataloguing in Publication Data
A catalogue record for this book is available from the British Library

Library of Congress Cataloging in Publication Data
Cuttle, Christopher.
Lighting design : a perception-based approach / Christopher Cuttle.
pages cm
Includes bibliographical references and index.
ISBN 978-0-415-73196-6 (hardback : alk. paper) -- ISBN 978-0-415-73197-3 (pbk. : alk. paper) -- ISBN 978-1-315-75688-2 (ebook) 1. Lighting, Architectural and decorative--Design. 2. Visual perception. I. Title.
NK2115.5.L5C88 2015
747'.92--dc23
2014009980

ISBN: 978-0-415-73196-6 (hbk)
ISBN: 978-0-415-73197-3 (pbk)
ISBN: 978-1-315-75688-2 (ebk)

Typeset in Bembo
by Saxon Graphics Ltd, Derby

Printed by Bell and Bain Ltd, Glasgow

CONTENTS

FIGURES

TABLES

ACKNOWLEDGEMENTS

The contents of this book have grown from the Advanced Lighting Design course that I have taught every year since 2005 at the Queensland University of Technology in Brisbane, Australia, for which I thank the programme coordinator, Professor Ian Cowling, and also the succession of lively and enquiring CPD (continuing professional development) students who have caused me to keep the curriculum in a state of continual revision.

While many people have contributed to the development of the ideas contained in this book, whether they realised it at the time or not, three former colleagues with whom I have maintained email contact have responded to specific issues that I encountered in preparing the text. They are, in no particular order, Joe Lynes and Professors Mark Rea and Peter Boyce. My thanks to each of them.

Those who have given permission for me to reproduce figures are acknowledged in the captions, but I want to make particular mention of Edward Adelson, Professor of Vision Science at the Massachusetts Institute of Technology, who not only permitted me to reproduce his Checker Shadow Illusion (Figure 1.1), but also two of my own modified versions of his brilliant figure.

INTRODUCTION

The aim of this book is to enable people who are familiar with the fundamentals of lighting technology to extend their activities into the field of lighting design. While the text is addressed primarily to students, it is relevant to professionals working in the fields of building services, interior design and architecture.

The premise of this book is that the key to lighting design is the skill to visualise the distribution of light within the volume of a space in terms of how it affects people's perceptions of the space and the objects (including the people) within it. The aim is not to produce lighting that will be noticed, but rather, to provide an envisioned balance of brightness that sets the appearance of individual objects into an overall design concept.

This is different from current notions of 'good lighting practice', which aim to provide for visibility, whereby 'visual tasks' may be performed efficiently and without promoting fatigue or discomfort. It is also quite different from some lighting design practice, where spectacular effects are achieved by treating the architecture as a backdrop onto which patterns of coloured light, or even brilliant images, are projected.

Several perception-based lighting concepts are introduced to enable distributions of illumination to be described in terms of how they may influence the appearance of a lit space. These descriptions involve perceived attributes of illumination, such as illumination that brings out 'colourfulness', or has a perceived 'flow', or perhaps 'sharpness'. It is shown that the three-dimensional distributions of illumination that underlie this understanding of lighting can be analysed in quantitative terms, enabling their characteristics to be measured and predicted. The principles governing these distributions are explained, and spreadsheets are used to automatically perform the calculations that relate perceived attributes to photometric quantities.

The objective is to enable a lighting designer to discuss lighting with clients and other professionals in terms of how illumination may influence the appearance of spaces and objects. When agreement is reached, the designer is then able to apply procedures that lead to layouts of luminaires and strategies for their control, and to do this with confidence that the envisioned appearance will be achieved.

1

THE ROLE OF VISUAL PERCEPTION

Chapter summary

The Checker Shadow Illusion demonstrates a clear distinction between the processes of vision and perception, where vision is concerned with discrimination of detail and perception involves recognition of surface and object attributes. The role of lighting in this recognition process involves the formation of lighting patterns created by interactions between objects and the surrounding light field. Confident recognition comprises clear perception of both object attributes and the light field. Three types of *object lighting patterns* are identified, being the shading, highlight, and shadow patterns, and it is by creating light fields that produce controlled balances of these three-dimensional lighting patterns that designers gain opportunities to influence how room surface and object attributes are likely to be perceived.

The evidence of your eyes

Figure 1.1 shows the Checker Shadow Illusion, and at first sight, the question has to be, where is the illusion? Everything looks quite normal. The answer lies in squares A and B: they are identical. That is to say, they are the same shade of grey and they have the same lightness, or to be more technical, they have the same reflectance (and thereby luminance) and the same chromaticity.

Do you find this credible? They certainly do not look the same. Now look at Figure 1.2, which shows a white sheet drawn over the figure with cut-outs for the two squares. Seen in this way they do look the same, and if you take a piece of card and punch a hole in it, you can slide it over the previous figure and convince yourself that the two squares are in fact identical and as shown in Figure 1.2.

This raises a question: how is it that, when the images of these two identical squares are simultaneously focussed onto the retina, in one case (Figure 1.2) they appear identical and in the other (Figure 1.1) they appear distinctly different?

FIGURE 1.1 The Checker Shadow Illusion. Squares A and B are identical. They are presented here as related colours, that is to say, they appear related to their surroundings. The lighting patterns that appear superimposed over the surrounding surfaces cause a viewer to perceive a 'flow' of light within the volume of this space, and which leads to the matching luminances of A and B being perceived quite differently. *(Source: en.wikipedia.org/wiki/Checker_shadow_illusion.html, downloaded January 2013)*

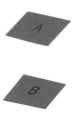

FIGURE 1.2 A white sheet has been drawn over the Checker Shadow Illusion, with cut-outs for squares A and B, and now they appear to be identical. In this case they are presented as unrelated colours.

Related and unrelated colours

The essential difference is that in Figure 1.1 the two squares are presented as *related colours*, that is to say, colours are perceived to belong to surfaces or objects seen in relation to other colours, and in Figure 1.2, they are shown as *unrelated colours*, meaning they are seen in isolation from other colours (Fairchild, 2005). As unrelated colours (grey is a colour), they are perceived to comprise nothing more than rectangular coloured shapes on a plain white background, but when they are set into the context of Figure 1.1, they are perceived as solid elements in a three-dimensional scene that have recognisable object attributes. It is this change in the way they are perceived that causes them to appear differently.

So what are the components of the surrounding scene that make this illusion so effective? Ask yourself, why is the cylindrical object there? Does it contribute something? In fact, it is a vital component of the illusion. So, what colour is it? Obviously, green. Is it uniformly green? Well, yes ... but look more carefully at the image of the object and you will see that both its greenness and its lightness vary hugely. The image is far from uniform, so how did you suppose the object to be uniformly green? The answer is that you perceived a distinctive lighting pattern superimposed over the uniformly green object. In Figure 1.3, the area enclosed by the object outline is shown as uniformly green and it appears as nothing more than a formless blob.

The solid, three-dimensional object perceived in Figure 1.1 is observed to be interacting with a directional 'flow' of light, which causes a *shading pattern* to be generated, and this appears superimposed over the green object surface. Note also that the cylinder's surface is not perfectly matt, and there is just a hint of a *highlight pattern* due to a specular component of reflection that is apparent at the rounded rim of the cylinder's top edge. These lighting patterns inform you about the object's attributes (Cuttle, 2008).

Now look at the checker board surface. Again we have a pattern due to the lighting, but in this case it is a *shadow pattern*, which has a different appearance from the shading

FIGURE 1.3   Previously the cylindrical object appeared to be uniformly green. Now it is uniformly green, but it does not look like a cylinder. That is because it is now lacking the lighting pattern due to interaction with the 'flow' of light.

and highlight patterns, but nonetheless is quite consistent with our perception of the overall 'flow' of light within the volume of the space. It will be obvious to you that if two surfaces have the same lightness (which also means they have the same reflectance) and one occurs within the shadow pattern and one outside it, they will have different luminance values. The creator of this brilliant illusion, Edward H. Adelson, Professor of Vision Science at the Massachusetts Institute of Technology, has carefully set it up so that squares A and B have the same luminance value, which means of course, that their images on your retina are identical. However, the function of the visual process is to provide information to the visual cortex of the brain, and here your perceptual process is telling you that, although these two squares match for luminance, they cannot have the same lightness. The one in the shadow must be lighter, that is to say, it must have higher reflectance, than the one in full light. You hold this innate understanding of lighting in your brain, and you cannot apply your conscious mind to overrule it.

In this way, it can be seen that the image focussed onto the retina is simply an optical projection of the visual scene that corresponds directly with the luminance and chromaticity values of the elements within the external scene. Since its inception, the study of lighting has concentrated on the visual process and how illumination may be applied to provide for visibility, later defined in terms of visual performance, but the role of vision is to serve the process of perception, and this occurs not at the retina, but in the visual cortex of the brain. What we perceive is not a pattern of brightness and colour, but a *gestalt*, this being a psychological term that describes the holistic entity that enables us to recognise all the forms and objects that make up our surroundings (Purves and Beau Lotto, 2003). Consciously, we are aware of three-dimensional spaces defined by surfaces and containing objects, but in order to make this much sense of the flow of information arriving through the optic nerve, we have to be subconsciously aware of a light field that fills the volume of the space. This is how we make sense of squares A and B. Seen in this way, it becomes obvious why attempts to analyse scenes in terms of luminance and chromaticity were bound to lead to frustration.

The role of ambient illumination

For most of the time, we live in a world of related colours. We are surrounded by surfaces and objects which, providing the entire scene is adequately illuminated, our perceptual faculties reliably recognise and make us aware of, sometimes so that we can cope with everyday life, and sometimes to elevate our senses to higher levels of appreciation, as when we encounter artworks or beauties of nature. Recognition involves identifying object attributes associated with all of the things that make up our surrounding environments, and our innate skill in doing this is truly impressive. Scientists working on artificial intelligence have tried to program super computers to perform in this way, but so far their best efforts fall far short of what human perception achieves every moment throughout our waking hours.

Provided that ambient illumination is sufficient, we are able to enter unfamiliar environments, orientate ourselves, and go about our business without hesitating to question the reliability of the perceptions we form of the surrounding environment. It is clear that substantial processing has to occur, very rapidly, between the retinal image and formation of the perception of the environment. There is no good reason why our perceptions of elements of the scene should show in-step correspondence with their photometric characteristics. Visual perception may be thought of as the process of making sense of the flow of sensory input through the optic nerve to the brain, where the purpose is to recognise surfaces and objects, rather than to record their images. Colours are perceived as related to object attributes, and effects of illumination are perceived as lighting patterns superimposed over them. As we recognised the cylinder in Figure 1.1 to be uniformly green with a superimposed shading pattern, so we also recognised the identical squares to differ in lightness because of the superimposed shadow pattern.

There will, however, be situations where we are confronted with elements seen in isolation from each other, and this is particularly likely to occur in conditions of low ambient illumination. When we find ourselves confronted by dark surroundings, reliance upon related colours and identification of object attributes may give way to perception of unrelated colours, and when this occurs, our perceptions do not distinguish lightness and illuminance separately, and luminance patterns dominate. That is to say, the appearances of individual objects within the scene relate to their brightness and chromaticity values, rather than upon recognition of their intrinsic attributes.

Figures 1.4 and 1.5 show two views of the same building. In Figure 1.4, we see a view of this magnificent cathedral in its setting, and we readily form a sense of its substantial mass and the materials from which it is constructed. Also, even if we are not conscious of it, we perceive the entire light field that generates this appearance. In Figure 1.5, our perception of this building is quite different. We have no notion of a natural light field, and the building seems to float, unattached to the ground. It is revealed by a glowing light pattern that does not distinguish between materials, and actually makes the building appear self-luminous. The building's appearance is dominated by brightness, and object attributes are not discernible. These two views show clearly the difference between related colours, in the daylight view, and unrelated colours in the night-time view. They also give us due appreciation of the role that lighting may play in bringing about fundamental differences in our perceptions.

Under normal daytime lighting, two-way interactions occur that enable our perceptual processes to make sense of the varied patterns of light and colour that are continuously being focussed onto our retinas. Working in one direction, there is the process of recognising object attributes that are revealed by the lighting patterns, while at the same time, and working in the opposite direction, it is the appearance of these lighting patterns that provides for the viewer's understanding of the light field that occupies the entire space.

FIGURE 1.4 The object attributes of this building are clearly recognisable, and the ambient illumination provides amply for all elements to appear as related colours. (Chartres Cathedral, France.)

FIGURE 1.5 The same building, but a vastly different appearance. Low ambient illumination provides a dark backdrop against which the cathedral glows with brightness. Object attributes are unrecognisable in this example of unrelated colours.

Perception as a basis for lighting design

From a design point of view, lighting practice may be seen to fall into two basic categories. On one hand, for illumination conditions ranging from outdoor daylight to indoor lighting where the ambient level is sufficient to avoid any appearance of gloom, we live in a world of related colours in which we distinguish readily between aspects of appearance that relate to the visible attributes of surfaces and objects, and aspects which relate to the lighting patterns that appear superimposed upon them.

On the other hand, in conditions of low ambient illumination, where we have a sense of darkness or even gloom, whether indoors or, most notably, outdoors at night, we typically experience unrelated colours and this may lead to the appearances of objects and surroundings dominated by brightness patterns that may offer no distinction between object lightness and surface illuminance.

The implications of this dichotomy for lighting design are profound. Outdoor night-time lighting practice, such as floodlighting and highway illumination, is based on creating brightness patterns that may bear little or no relationship to surface or object properties. Alternatively, for situations where ambient illumination is at least sufficient to maintain an appearance of adequacy (apart from outdoor daylight, this may be taken to include all indoor spaces where the illumination complies with current standards for general lighting practice) we take in entire visual scenes including object attributes, and involving instant recognition of familiar objects and scrutiny of unfamiliar or otherwise interesting objects. The identification of object attributes may become a matter of keen interest, as when admiring an art object or seeking to detect a flaw in a manufactured product, and we depend upon the lighting patterns to enable us to discriminate and to respond to differences of object attributes.

Between these two sets of conditions is a range in which some uncertainty prevails. We have, for example, all experienced 'tricks of the light' that can occur at twilight, and generally, recommendations for good lighting practice aim to avoid such conditions. Perhaps surprisingly, it is within this range that lighting designers achieve some of their most spectacular display effects. By isolating specific objects from their backgrounds and illuminating them from concealed light sources, lighting can be applied to alter the appearance of selected object attributes, such as making selected objects appear more textured, or colourful, or glossy. All of this thinking will be developed in following chapters.

Before we close this chapter, ask yourself, why do we call Figure 1.1 an illusion? If the page is evenly illuminated, squares A and B will have the same luminance and so they stimulate their corresponding areas of our retinas to the same level. The fact that these equal stimuli do not correspond to equal sensations of brightness is cited as an illusion. The point needs to be made that vision serves the process of perception, and perception is not concerned with assessing or responding to luminance. Its role is to continually seek to recognise object attributes from the flow of data arriving from the eyes. When we are confronted with Figure 1.1 in a condition of adequate illumination, our perception process performs its task to perfection. A is correctly recognised as a dark checker board square, and B as a light square. Rather than labelling Figure 1.1 as an illusion, perhaps we should refer to it as an insight into the workings of the visual perception process.

However, the real purpose for examining this image has been to show how perception depends upon and is influenced by the lighting patterns that objects and surfaces generate through interactions with their surrounding light fields. These lighting patterns may have the effects of revealing, subduing, or enhancing selected object attributes, and it is through control of light field distributions that lighting designers influence people's perceptions of object attributes. Skill in exercising this control, particularly for indoor lighting, is the essence of lighting design and the central theme of this book.

References

Cuttle, C. (2008). *Lighting by Design, Second Edition.* Oxford: Architectural Press.
Fairchild, M.D. (2005). *Color Appearance Models, Second Edition.* Chichester: Wiley.
Purves, D. and R. Beau Lotto (2003). *Why we see what we do: An empirical theory of vision.* Sunderland, MA: Sinauer Associates.

2

AMBIENT ILLUMINATION

Chapter summary

The perception of ambient illumination concerns whether a space appears to be brightly lit, dimly lit, or something in between. At first this might seem a rather superficial observation until we consider all of the associations that we have with 'bright light' and 'dim light', at which point ambient illumination becomes a key lighting design concept. It provides a basis for planning lighting based on the perceived difference of illumination between adjacent areas, or spaces seen in sequence as when passing through a building. A thought experiment is introduced which leads to the conclusion that mean room surface exitance (MRSE) provides a useful indicator of ambient illumination, where MRSE is a measure of inter-reflected light from surrounding room surfaces, excluding direct light from windows or luminaires. The Ambient Illumination spreadsheet facilitates application of this concept.

The amount of light

An important decision in lighting design is, 'What appearance of overall brightness (or dimness) is this space to have?' General lighting practice gives emphasis to the issue of how much light must be provided to enable people to perform the visual tasks associated with whatever activity occurs within the space and, of course, this must always be kept in mind. In a banking hall, for example, we need to ensure that the counters are lit to an illuminance that is sufficient to enable the tellers to perform their work throughout the working day without suffering strain. While that aspect of illumination must not be overlooked, there is an overarching design decision to be made, which is whether the overall appearance of the space is to be a bright, lively and stimulating environment, or whether a more dim overall appearance is wanted. The aim of a dim appearance may be to present a subdued, and perhaps sombre, appearance, or alternatively, to create a setting in which illumination can be directed onto selected targets to present them in high contrast relative to their surroundings. Of course, the surroundings cannot be made too dim as illumination must always be sufficient for safe movement, but there is substantial scope for a designer to choose whether, in a particular situation, the overall impression is to be of a bright space, or of a dim space, or of something in between. Clearly, the impressions that visitors would form of the space will be substantially affected by the designer's decision.

This raises a question. If we are not lighting a visual task plane for visibility, but are instead illuminating a space for a certain appearance of overall brightness, how do we specify the level of illumination that will achieve this objective? All around the world, lighting standards, codes, and recommended practice documents specify illumination levels for various indoor activities in terms of illuminance (lux) and a uniformity factor. If someone states that 'This is a 400 lux installation', that means that illuminance values measured on the horizontal working plane, usually specified as being 700mm above floor level and extending from wall to wall within the space, should average at least 400 lux, and furthermore, at no point should illuminance drop to less than 80 per cent of that average value.

The reasons for this are historical. It was in the late nineteenth century that the practice of measuring illumination emerged, and for indoor lighting, the prime purpose was to enable working people to remain productive for the full duration of the working day, despite daylight fluctuations. While the recommended illuminance levels have increased more than tenfold since those days, the measurement procedures are essentially unchanged even though light meters have undergone substantial development. The two specified measures, an average illuminance and the uniformity factor, are the means by which lighting quantity is specified, and more than that, they govern how people think about illumination quantity. Perhaps the worst feature of these specifications is that they have the effect of inhibiting exploration of different ways in which the light might be distributed in a space, and how lighting may be applied to create a lit appearance that relates to a space and the objects it contains. For lighting designers, these aspects of appearance are all-important, and in fact, it may be said that they form the very basis of what lighting design is all about. To be obliged to ensure that all lighting is 'code compliant' is nothing short of a denial to pursue the most fundamental lighting design objectives.

A thought experiment

We are going to conduct a thought experiment as a first step to exploring how lighting does more than simply make things visible, and in fact, we are going to explore how lighting affects the appearance of everything we see. To start, you need to get yourself into an experimental mindset. The first requirement is to forget everything you know. Then, imagine an indoor space where the sum total of ceiling, wall and floor areas add up to $100m^2$, as shown in Figure 2.1.

Then, into this space is added a luminaire that emits a total a luminous flux, F, of 5000 lumens (Figure 2.2).

How brightly lit will the space appear? This might seem to be a difficult question to answer, which is as it should be because a vital piece of information is lacking. Until the room surface reflectance values are specified, you have no way of knowing how much light there is in this space.

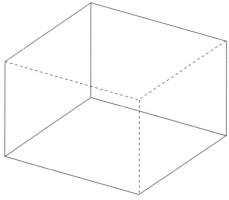

Room surface area A = 100m²

FIGURE 2.1   To start the thought experiment, imagine a room for which the sum of ceiling, walls, and floor area is 100m².

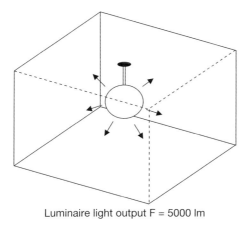

Luminaire light output F = 5000 lm

FIGURE 2.2   To the room is added a luminaire with a total flux output F = 5000 lumens.

To keep life simple, we will specify that all room surfaces have a reflectance value, ρ_{rs}, of 0.5, that is to say, 50 per cent of incident lumens are absorbed and 50 per cent are reflected (Figure 2.3). Now we can work out how many lumens there are in the space.

How much light do we have?

	addition	total
Initial flux (F)	5000	5000
First reflection	2500	7500
Second reflection	1250	8750
Third reflection	625	9375
and so on …		

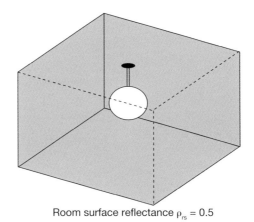

Room surface reflectance ρ_{rs} = 0.5

FIGURE 2.3 All room surfaces are given a neutral grey finish so that ρ_{rs} = 0.5.

All of the initial 5000 lumens from the luminaire are incident on room surfaces that reflect 50 per cent back into the space, so the first reflection adds 2500 lm, bringing the total luminous flux in the space up to 7500 lm. These reflected lumens are again incident on room surfaces, and the second reflection adds another 1250 lumens to the total. The process repeats, so that you could go on adding reflected components of the initial flux until they become insignificantly small. Alternatively, the effect of an infinite number of reflections is given by dividing the initial flux by $(1 - \rho)$, so that:

$$\text{Total flux} = F/(1 - \rho)$$
$$= 5000/(1 - 0.5)$$
$$= \textit{10,000 lumens}$$

An interesting point emerges here. We have surrounded the luminaire with surfaces that reflect 50 per cent of the light back into the space, and this has doubled the number of lumens. Keep this point in mind. Now we divide the total flux by the total room surface area to get the average room surface illuminance:

$$E_{rs} = 10,000/100$$
$$= 100 \text{ lux}$$

At last we have a measure we can understand. This would be enough light for us to see our way around the space, but not enough to make the room appear brightly lit. Let's suppose that we want a reasonably bright appearance. Well, we could fit a bigger lamp in the luminaire, but before we take that easy option, let's think a bit more about the effect of room surface reflectance. We have seen that it can have a quite surprising effect on the overall amount of light in the space.

What would be the effect of increasing ρ_{rs} to 0.8, as shown in Figure 2.4? Combining the expressions we used before, it follows that the mean room surface illuminance:

$$E_{rs} = \frac{F}{A(1-\rho)}$$

$$= \frac{5000}{100(1-0.8)}$$

$$= \underline{250 \text{ lux}}$$

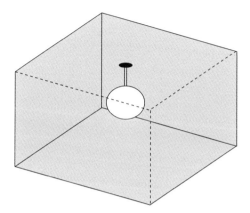

Room surface reflectance $\rho_{rs} = 0.8$

FIGURE 2.4 Room surface reflectance is increased so that $\rho_{rs} = 0.8$.

This deserves some careful attention. We increased ρ_{rs} from 0.5 to 0.8, which is a 60 per cent increase, and the total flux increased two-and-a-half times! How can this be so? Think about it this way. It is conventional to refer to surface reflectance values, but try thinking instead of surface absorptance values, where $\alpha = (1 - \rho)$. What we have done has been to reduce α_{rs} from 0.5 to 0.2, and that is where the 2.5 factor comes from.

As this is a thought experiment, think about what would happen if we could reduce α_{rs} to zero. Well, the lumens would just keep bouncing around inside the room. When you switched on the luminaire, the total flux would keep on increasing. If you did not switch off in time, the room probably would explode! If you did switch off in time, the light level would remain constant. You could come back a month later and it would be undiminished, until you open the door and in a flash all the lumens pour out and the room would be in darkness. Thought experiments really can be fun. Now think about going in the opposite direction.

What would be the effect of reducing ρ_{rs} to zero? How brightly lit would the room appear? The question is of course meaningless. The only thing visible would be the luminaire, as shown in Figure 2.5. If you were sufficiently adventurous, you could feel your way around the room and you could use a light meter to confirm the value of the mean room surface illuminance:

$$E_{rs} = \frac{F}{A(1-\rho)}$$

$$= \frac{5000}{100(1-0)}$$

$$= \underline{50 \text{ lux}}$$

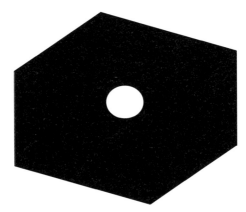

Room surface reflectance $\rho_{rs} = 0$

FIGURE 2.5   Room surface reflectance is reduced to zero, so $\rho_{rs} = 0$.

The meter would respond to those 50 lux, but your eye would not. Here is another important point. The direct flux from the luminaire has no effect on the appearance of the room. It is not until the flux has undergone at least one reflection that it makes any contribution towards our impression of how brightly, or dimly, lit the room appears. To have a useful measure of how the ambient illumination affects the appearance of a room, we need to ignore direct light and take account only of reflected light.

Let's think now about a general expression for ambient illumination as it may affect our impression of the brightness of an enclosed space. The luminaire is to be ignored, and so in Figure 2.6, it is shown black. Admittedly, a black luminaire emitting 5000 lm is rather more demanding of the imagination, but bear with the idea. To take account of only light reflected from room surfaces, we need an expression for *mean room surface exitance, MRSE*, where exitance expresses the average density of luminous flux exiting, or emerging from, a surface in lumens per square metre, lm/m^2.

$$MRSE = \frac{F\rho}{A(1-\rho)} \tag{2.1}$$

$$= \frac{FRF}{A\alpha} \tag{2.2}$$

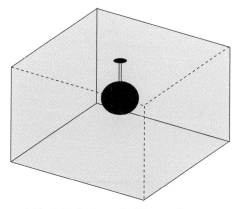

A black luminaire emits F lumens in a room
of area A and reflectance ρ

FIGURE 2.6 The final stage of the thought experiment. A black luminaire emits F lm in a room of area A and uniform surface reflectance ρ, and mean room surface exitance, MRSE, is predictable from Formulae 2.1 and 2.2.

The upper line of Formula 2.2 is the *first reflected flux FRF*, which is the initial flux after it has undergone its first reflection. This is the energy that initiates the inter-reflection process that makes the spaces we live in luminous. More descriptively, it is sometimes referred to as the 'first bounce' lumens.

The bottom line is the *room absorption, Aα*. One square metre of perfectly black surface would comprise $1.0m^2$ of room absorption; alternatively, it may comprise $2.0m^2$ of a material for which $α = 0.5$, or again, $4.0m^2$ if $α = 0.25$. It is a fact that when you walk into a room, the ambient illumination reduces because you have increased the room absorption. You could minimise that effect by wearing white clothing, but that is unlikely to catch on among lighting designers. My own observation is that if lighting designers can be said to have a uniform, it is black. It seems we aspire to be perfect light absorbers!

The MRSE concept

Of course, real rooms do not have uniform reflectance values, but this can be coped with without undue complication.

On the top line of Formula 2.1, Fρ is the First Reflected Flux, FRF, which is the sum of 'first bounce' lumens from all of the room surfaces, such as ceiling, walls, partitions and any other substantial objects in the room. It is obtained by summing the products of:

- direct illuminance of each surface $E_{s(d)}$
- surface area A_s
- surface reflectance $ρ_s$

So, in a room having n surface elements:

$$\text{FRF} = \sum_{s=1}^{n} E_{s(d)} \cdot A_s \cdot \rho_s \tag{2.3}$$

On the bottom line of Formula 2.1, $A(1 - \rho)$ is the Room Absorption, indicated by the symbol $A\alpha$, and it is a measure of the room's capacity to absorb light. As it is conventional to describe surfaces in terms of reflectance rather than absorptance;

$$A\alpha = \sum_{s=1}^{n} A_s (1 - \rho_s) \tag{2.4}$$

The general expression for mean room surface exitance, Formula 2.2, may be summarised as:

The mean room surface exitance equals the first bounce lumens divided by the room absorption.

MRSE has three valuable uses:

1   The MRSE value provides an indication of the *perceived brightness or dimness of ambient illumination*. Table 2.1 gives an approximate guide for the two decades of ambient illumination that cover the range of indoor general lighting practice. These values are based on various studies conducted by the author and reported by other researchers, and it should be noted that ambient illumination relates to a perceived effect, while MRSE is a measurable illumination quantity, like illuminance, but not to be confused with working plane illuminance.

TABLE 2.1 Perceived brightness or dimness of ambient illumination

Mean room surface exitance (MRSE, lm/m²)	Perceived brightness or dimness of ambient illumination
10	Lowest level for reasonable colour discrimination
30	Dim appearance
100	Lowest level for 'acceptably bright' appearance
300	Bright appearance
1000	Distinctly bright appearance

2   The MRSE ratio for adjacent spaces provides an index of the *perceived difference of illumination*. Table 2.2 gives an approximate guide for this perceived difference as one moves from space to space within a building, or to the appearance of differently

TABLE 2.2 Perceived differences of exitance or illuminance

Exitance or illuminance ratio	Perceived difference
1.5:1	Noticeable
3:1	Distinct
10:1	Strong
40:1	Emphatic

illuminated surfaces or objects within a space. There is more about this perceived difference effect in the following chapter.

3   It may provide an acceptable measure of the total *indirect illuminance* received by an object or surface within the space, so that for a surface S, the total surface illuminance may be approximately estimated by the formula:

$$E_s = E_{s(d)} + MRSE \qquad\qquad (2.5)$$

where $E_{s(d)}$ is the direct illuminance of surface S. Procedures for predicting direct illumination are explained in Chapter 6.

Before we examine how MRSE may be applied in the design process, I am conscious that some readers may be finding the exitance term unfamiliar, as it often is customary to refer to illuminance as the metric for incident light, and luminance for reflected light. To see where exitance fits in, take a step back. Illuminance is a simple concept. It refers to the density of luminous flux incident on a surface, either at a point or over an area, in lux, where 1 lux equals 1 lumen per square metre (lm/m^2). Exitance is also a simple concept. It refers to the density of flux exiting, or emerging from, a surface in lm/m^2. (It should be noted that the lux unit is defined as the unit of illuminance, and so should not be used for exitance. Actually, keeping these units distinct for incident and exiting flux helps to avoid confusion.) Now consider luminance. This is not a simple concept. As simply as I can express it, it is the luminous flux due to a small element in a given direction, relative to the area of the element projected in that direction and the solid angle subtending the flux, measured in candelas per square metre (cd/m^2). It needs to be recognised that there are times when it is necessary to use the luminance metric, as for visual task analysis where the contrast of the critical detail has to be defined, but to refer to the average luminance of a wall or a ceiling really is meaningless without a defined view point. After all, what is the average projected area of one of these elements? Readers who are not familiar with the exitance term are strongly advised to make themselves acquainted with it. Not only is it a much more simple concept than luminance, but when we are concerned how illumination affects the appearance of room surfaces, it is the correct term to use. Seen in this way, MRSE is the measure of the overall density of inter-reflected light within the volume of an enclosed space.

Applying the ambient illumination concept in design

Room surface reflectances are so influential upon both the appearance of indoor spaces and the distribution of illumination within them that, in an ideal world, lighting designers would take control of them. The reality is that generally someone else will make those decisions, but lighting designers must persist in making these decision makers aware of the influence they exert over ambient illumination and the overall appearance of the illuminated space.

The creativity of a lighting designer is largely determined by the ability to perceive a space and its objects *in light*, and as we have seen, the perceived light is reflected (not direct) light. A room in which high reflectance surfaces face other high reflectance surfaces is one in which inter-reflected flux persists, and it is this inter-reflected flux that provides for our sense of how brightly or dimly lit the space appears.

To initiate this inter-reflected flux, direct light, which travels from source to receiving surface without visible effect, has to be applied. The essential skill of a lighting designer may be seen as the ability to devise an invisible distribution of direct flux that will generate an envisaged distribution of reflected flux.

Large, high reflectance surfaces enable the direct light to be applied efficiently and unobtrusively, and where high MRSE levels are to be provided, the availability of large, light-coloured surfaces that can be washed with light becomes an important consideration for both appearance and energy efficiency. Conversely, where the aim is to keep MRSE low, perhaps to provide high contrasts for display lighting, dark-coloured room surfaces reinforce the visual effect by absorbing both spill light (display lighting that misses the display) and 'first bounce lumens' reflected from the displays.

Estimating surface reflectance values is not straightforward. The Munsell Value (MV) scale orders surface colours on a 10-step scale according to lightness assessments, where MV0 appears to be a perfect black, and MV10 a perfect white. Unlike reflectance, lightness is a subjective scale, and while it relates to reflectance, the relationship is far from linear. A value of MV5 is perceptually mid-way between black and white and so it might be expected to have a reflectance around 0.5, but as Figure 2.7 shows, its actual value is

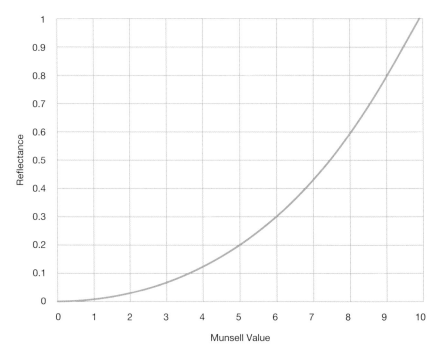

FIGURE 2.7 Reflectance plotted against Munsell Value, where a surface of MV0 would be assessed as a perfect black and MV10 as a perfect white. Perceptually MV5 is mid-way between these extremes and might be expected to have a reflectance of 0.5, but actually, it has a reflectance of approximately 0.2.

approximately 0.2. Furthermore, it can be seen that a surface having a reflectance of 0.5 has a MV of approximately 7.5, and that puts it perceptually three-quarters of the way towards perfect white. The practical implication of this pronounced non-linearity is that inexperienced designers are inclined to substantially overestimate reflectance values. A reasonably reliable procedure is to fit an internally blackened tube over an illuminance meter as shown in Figure 2.8 and to take two readings, one for the surface, R_S and one for a sheet of good quality white paper which has been slid over the surface, R_p. It is reasonable to assume that the paper has a reflectance of 0.9, so that for a measure of surface reflectance, $\rho_S = 0.9\,R_S/R_p$. Patterned as well as plain surfaces can be dealt with in this way, but care needs to be taken to avoid specular reflections, particularly for glossy surfaces. Also, it should not be assumed that shiny surfaces have high reflectance. These surfaces simply reflect without diffusion, so that if the meter is exposed to specular reflection, what is being measured is an image of a light source rather than the overall reflection of light from the surface.

FIGURE 2.8 Using an internally blackened tube mounted onto a light meter to obtain a measurement of surface reflectance. Two measurements are made without moving the meter, one of the surface as shown, and a comparison reading with a sheet of white paper in the measurement zone.

The effects of this tendency to overestimate reflectance values are compounded by the impact of surface reflectance values on MRSE. It can be seen from Formula 2.1 that MRSE is proportional to the ratio of room surface reflectance to absorptance, ρ/α. Figure 2.9 plots the value of this ratio relative to reflectance, and again it can be seen that the impact of room surface reflectance increases exponentially with reflectance, and could lead to grossly inflated MRSE values being predicted where reflectance values have been overestimated. We can see here the effects of reflectance that were observed in the thought experiment, and while these effects are real, they will not be realized unless reflectance values have been accurately assessed.

These considerations suggest an initial sequence for applying these concepts:

1   Decide upon the level of MRSE, taking account of design considerations concerning the perceived brightness or dimness of ambient illumination, and referring to Table 2.1 and the discussion in the section entitled 'The amount of light'.
2   Calculate the room absorption, $A\alpha$, referring to Formula 2.4.
3   Determine the level of first reflected flux, turning Formula 2.2 around to $FRF = MRSE \times A\alpha$
4   Determine a distribution of direct flux to provide the FRF value. At this point, we come to a central design issue: how to distribute the direct flux, $F_{s(d)}$, or in other words, how to choose the surfaces onto which flux will be directed. To explain this issue we will consider two cases.

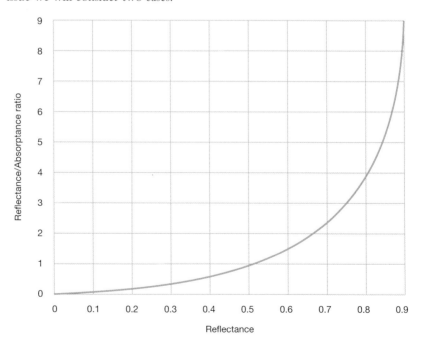

FIGURE 2.9   The value of the reflectance/absorptance ratio is proportional to mean room surface exitance, MRSE. Note how values increase exponentially at higher reflectance values.

Throughout this book we will be making use of spreadsheets to facilitate calculations, and their outputs are shown in the Boxes alongside the text. Readers are strongly encouraged to follow the instructions for downloading the spreadsheets so they can then follow the applications described. Boxes 2.1 and 2.2 show two outputs of the Ambient Illumination Spreadsheet, but the real benefit of doing calculations in this way is not that it all happens so quickly and easily (although that undoubtedly is a benefit) but that, once a situation has been set up, the user is able to explore alternative solutions with instant feedback. Readers are strongly encouraged to follow these examples, and then to go beyond them by asking, 'What if …?'

BOX 2.1

AMBIENT ILLUMINATION

140117

Project   Case 1

MRSE   150 lm/m^2

Room Dimensions

Length	Width	Height
12	9	3 m

Surface	As	ρs	Aαs	Direct Flux (%)	$F_{s(d)}$	E_s	E_s/MRSE
Ceiling	108	0.85	16.2	75	24437	376	2.5
Walls	126	0.5	63	15	4887	189	1.3
Floor	108	0.25	81	10	3258	180	1.2
Object 1	0	0	0	0	0	0	0.0
Object 2	0	0	0	0	0	0	0.0
Object 3	0	0	0	0	0	0	0.0

Room absorption Aα   160.2 m^2

First reflected flux (FRF)   24030 lm

Total luminaire flux (F)   32583 lm

Key

ρs	Reflectance of surface S
Aαs	Absorption of surface S (m^2)
As	Area of surface S (m^2)
E_s	Illuminance of surface S (lx)
$F_{s(d)}$	Direct flux incident on surface S (lm)
MRSE	Mean room surface exitance (lm/m^2)

Notes

Enter data only in cells shown in red – all other data are calculated automatically.
Direct Flux (%) is the direct flux incident on S as a percentage of total luminous flux.

Envisage an indoor space measuring 12m long, 9m wide, and 3m high. To keep life simple, we will not get too specific about the function of this room. For Case 1 we will work on the basis that the aim is to provide a fairly bright overall appearance, where everything appears adequately lit but no objects are to be selected for particular attention, and what is called for is a well-diffused, overall illumination. Decisions have been made for surface finishes, and it has been agreed that ceiling reflectance, ρ_{clg}, is to be 0.85, ρ_{wall} to have a value of 0.5, and ρ_{flr} will be 0.25, and Box 2.1 shows the dimensions and the reflectances entered on the Ambient Illumination Spreadsheet.

After giving due consideration to the points discussed in 'The amount of light', we decide upon a MRSE level of 150 lm/m². This value is entered on the spreadsheet, noting that data are to be entered only into cells marked in red. To fully understand the procedure, the reader is advised to check the calculation on paper using the aforementioned formulae.

The FRF value shown in Box 2.1 is the number of lumens reflected from all of the room surfaces required to provide the moderately bright overall appearance that we have set as our goal. Now we address the first really important design issue: how to distribute the direct flux? The aim is to achieve a well-diffused illumination, and to do this without creating distinctly bright zones suggests a lighting installation that distributes illumination evenly over large surfaces. The only remaining red values are in the Direct Flux (%) column, and this is the column where the designer experiments with direct flux distributions. Two values have been entered: 15 per cent of total luminaire output is to be directed onto the walls, and 10 per cent onto the floor. As no objects have been entered, that leaves 75 per cent onto the ceiling. The next column, $F_{s(d)}$, shows the number of lumens of direct flux required on each room surface; next, the E_s column shows the illuminance (including indirect flux) on each surface; and in the final column, the ratios of surface illuminance to ambient illuminance, E_s/MRSE. Below these columns are the values of $A\alpha$, FRF and the total luminous flux, F, to be emitted by the luminaires.

Ways of predicting luminaire layouts for direct light distributions are explained in Chapter 6, but before that, this spreadsheet gives the designer opportunity to explore the implications of flux distribution. To experience this, download the Ambient Illumination spreadsheet and click the Box 2.1 tag. Try changing the walls and floor flux percentages, and if you like, you can add a few objects, such as furniture items. You will see that every time you add more room absorption or direct more flux onto surfaces of lower reflectance, up goes the luminaire flux. For optimum energy efficiency, set the walls and floor direct flux percentages to zero so that the direct ceiling flux becomes 100 per cent, and you will see the luminaire flux drop to just over 28,000 lm. This would be the most energy efficient solution for achieving the MRSE target in this location, but when this happens, the value of E_s/MRSE climbs to 2.7, and this may be a cause for concern.

If the aim is to achieve the ambient illumination without any surface appearing noticeably more strongly lit than any other surface, then as indicated in Table 2.2, the aim should be to keep values of E_s/MRSE below 1.5. A value of 2.7 for the ceiling indicates that this surface will appear distinctly more strongly lit than any other surface or object in this space, and in fact, for the case shown in Box 2.1, where some flux is directed onto the walls and floor, the E_s/MRSE value is only slightly reduced to 2.5, so the appearance of the direct illumination onto the ceiling would certainly be 'noticeable', even if not 'distinct'. We could try adjusting the percentage values on the spreadsheet to achieve a less pronounced effect, but watch the value of the total luminaire flux, F. As more luminaire flux is directed onto lower reflectance surfaces, so the flux required to provide the MRSE value goes up. It should not pass notice that this flies in the face of conventional practice. All around the world, lighting standards for illumination sufficiency for indoor activities are specified in terms of illuminance applied onto the horizontal working plane, from which it follows that 'efficient' lighting takes the form of a grid layout of luminaires that directs its output directly onto that plane. While it is widely acknowledged that indirect ceiling lighting installations can achieve pleasant effects, the way the standards are specified causes them to be classified as inefficient. When a designer is satisfied that a satisfactory distribution of direct flux has been achieved, a copy of the spreadsheet would be saved onto the design project file.

Now turn attention to Case 2, for which we have a quite different aim. Again, we will not get too specific about the situation, but this time the aim is that a few selected objects are to be presented for display, and these are to become the 'targets' for the lighting with the intention that they will catch attention by appearing brightly lit in a dim setting. The revised output for the Ambient Illumination spreadsheet is shown in Box 2.2, and it shows that most of the direct flux is to be directed onto these targets. Even so, this is a space that people would need to be able to find their way through, so a background of inky blackness would not be acceptable. This brings us face-to-face with a tricky design decision. On one hand we aim to achieve a luminous environment that is dark enough to provide for effective display contrasts, while on the other hand it needs to be light enough for people to find their way through safely, and, at least as important, we need to create an entry to the space that people find welcoming. We should keep in mind that in order to attract people to enter this dim space, at least part of the displayed material should be positioned so that it is visible to someone approaching the entrance to the space.

As shown in Box 2.2, we have opted for a MRSE level of 10 lm/m^2, and at this stage we enter into discussion with the design team. It is agreed that both ρ_{clg} and ρ_{flr} are to be kept down to a level of 0.15, although to provide a slightly lighter background to the displays, a wall finish with a reflectance value of 0.25 is chosen. The displayed objects have a total surface area of $20m^2$ with an average reflectance of 0.35, but it would be unrealistic to suppose that we will be able to direct 100 per cent of the luminaire flux onto them. It has been assumed that there will be 10 per cent spill light, half of it onto the walls and half onto the floor, and based on all these inputs, the spreadsheet shows that we need a total luminaire flux of 8690 lumens. That luminous flux, appropriately directed, will provide a display illuminance of 401 lux, and, referring again to Table 2.2, the visual effect will be 'emphatic', as it will provide a E_s/MRSE value of 40. Note that in order to achieve this dramatic effect we did not start by setting the target illuminance, but rather, we set the ambient illuminance and then determined the flux distribution. To provide a higher level of target illuminance would have the effect of raising the ambient illumination above the design value without adding to the E_s/MRSE ratio.

From these two cases it can be seen that in order for lighting to exert its potential for influencing the appearance of everything we see, control over room surface reflectance values is as important as being able to control direct flux distributions. Between these two quite extreme cases, many options exist for designers to control ambient illumination level to support chosen lighting design objectives. The Ambient Illumination Spreadsheet is a useful tool for achieving this control.

BOX 2.2

AMBIENT ILLUMINATION SPREADSHEET

140117

Project   Case 2

MRSE   10 lm/m^2

Room Dimensions

Length	Width	Height
12	9	3 m

Surface	As	ρs	Aαs	Direct Flux (%)	$F_{s(d)}$	E_s	E_s/MRSE
Ceiling	108	0.15	91.8	0	0	10	1.0
Walls	126	0.25	94.5	5	435	13	1.3
Floor	108	0.15	91.8	5	435	14	1.4
Object 1	20	0.35	13	90	7821	401	40.1
Object 2	0	0	0	0	0	0	0.0
Object 3	0	0	0	0	0	0	0.0

Room absorption Aα   291.1 m^2

First reflected flux (FRF)   2911 lm

Total luminaire flux (F)   8690 lm

Key		Notes
ρs	Reflectance of surface S	Enter data only in cells shown in red – all other data are calculated automatically.
Aαs	Absorption of surface S (m^2)	
As	Area of surface S (m^2)	Direct Flux (%) is the direct flux incident on S as a percentage of total luminous flux.
E_s	Illuminance of surface S (lx)	
$F_{s(d)}$	Direct flux incident on surface S (lm)	
MRSE	Mean room surface exitance (lm/m^2)	

3

ILLUMINATION HIERARCHIES

Chapter summary

Where ambient illumination is sufficient for illuminance and lightness (which is related to reflectance) to be perceived separately, as typically occurs for conventional indoor lighting practice, lighting may be planned in terms of illuminance (rather than luminance) distributions. Local concentrations of illumination can be applied to direct attention, to give emphasis and identify objects that the designer deems to be visually significant. The notion of ordered distributions of illumination leads to the concept of illumination hierarchy, whereby illumination distributions are structured as a principal means by which the designer may express his or her design intentions. Such distributions are planned as changing balances of direct and indirect illumination, and are achieved by specifying *target/ambient illuminance ratio* (TAIR) values. The Illumination Hierarchy spreadsheet facilitates application of this concept.

Ordered illumination distributions

Most forms of life are attracted towards light, and humans are no exception. Phototropism is the process by which attention is drawn toward the brightest part of the field of view. It can be detrimental, as when a glare source creates a conflict between itself and what a person wants to see, and in general lighting practice much attention is given to avoiding such effects. However, for lighting designers it is a powerful tool, enabling us to draw attention to what we want people to notice and away from things of secondary or tertiary significance. An ordered illumination distribution is the underpinning basis for structuring a lighting design concept.

It is important to spend some time looking carefully at how our perceptions of space and objects are influenced by selective illumination. It was noted in Chapter 1 that colours that make up an overall scene are generally perceived as *related colours,* and as long as illumination is sufficient to ensure photopic adaptation, we have no difficulty in recognising all the surrounding surfaces and objects that make up our environments. The process of recognising the multitude of 'things' that may, at any time, comprise our surroundings falls within the topic of perceptual psychology, but without getting involved in that field of learning it is sufficient here to acknowledge that this recognition process involves discriminating differences of object attributes such as lightness, hue and saturation, from which we form perceptions of spaces, people, and objects. We achieve this without conscious effort throughout our waking hours over a very wide range of 'adequate' lighting conditions. In this context, the onset of dimness may be thought of as the borderline of reliable recognition of object attributes.

However, with ordered illumination distributions we can go beyond simply providing for object recognition. Retailers long ago worked out that if an object that is small in relation to its surroundings receives selective illumination, particularly without the source of light being evident, people's perceptions of that object's attributes can be significantly affected. Whether or not it appears more brightly lit, it is likely to appear more colourful, and perhaps more textured or more glossy, than it would appear without selective illumination. Lighting designers have at their disposal the means to establish hierarchies of visual significance in illuminated scenes, and means for achieving this in an ordered manner is the content of this chapter.

Illuminance ratios

When we place an attractive object, such as a vase of flowers, beside a window to 'catch the light', we are exploiting the potential for a pool of local illumination to identify this object as having been selected for special attention. Similarly, electric lighting can provide a planned gradation of illumination that expresses the designer's concept of layers of difference. Hard-edged contrasts can give emphasis to such effects, but alternatively, a different but equally striking effect may be achieved by a build-up of illuminance that leads the eye progressively towards the designer's objective. High drama requires that surroundings are cast into gloom, but in architectural situations, safety requirements generally require surroundings to remain visible, although perhaps distinctly dim, at all times. Planning such distributions is more than simply selecting a few objects for spotlighting. It involves devising an ordered distribution of lighting to achieve an *illumination hierarchy*.

The concept of a structured illumination distribution was pioneered by J.M. Waldram (1954). Working from a perspective sketch of the location, he would assign an 'apparent brightness' value to each significant element of the view, and then he would convert those subjective values into luminance values so that he could apply illumination engineering procedures to determine a suitable flux distribution. Waldram's notion of creating an ordered brightness distribution related to luminance would seem to be valid for low adaptation situations, such as occur in outdoor lighting, but not for situations where surface lightness is readily recognised, such as in adequately illuminated indoor scenes. As has been noted, for these situations our perceptions distinguish illumination differences more or less independently of surface reflectance values.

J.A. Lynes (1987) has proposed a design approach based on Waldram's method with the difference that the designer develops a structured distribution of surface illuminance values. Lynes introduces his students to the topic through an exercise in perceived difference of illumination, and his simple procedure is illustrated in Figure 3.1. He stands in front of his class with a spotlight shining onto a white screen. Point 0 is the brightest spot, and from this point a numbered scale extends across the screen. Each student completes a score card, and starts by indicating the scale value that, in his or her assessment, corresponds to the point along the scale at which a 'noticeable difference of brightness' occurs. This is the student's 'N' value, and would be followed by a 'D' value for a distinct difference, an 'S' value for a strong difference and an 'E' value for an emphatic difference. The cards are then gathered, average values calculated and consensus values for N, D, S and E are marked on the screen. After that, Lynes measures the illuminance level at each point, from which illuminance ratios are calculated for each perceived difference.

The author has conducted this exercise with students on numerous occasions. Perhaps the first surprise is to find how easy it is to obtain consensus, and the second is how well the results are repeated year after year. The data presented in Table 2.2 is typical, and while this simple procedure may not qualify as 'good science', it is well worth going through the procedure. It calls for thoughtful observation, and, perhaps surprisingly, it provides useful guidance for lighting design. Not only students, but anyone interested in designing lighting should go through the process of making these illumination difference assessments at least once during their lifetime.

Whereas in Chapter 2 we discussed how initial responses to a space may be influenced by ambient illumination, now we turn attention to the perceived effects that can be

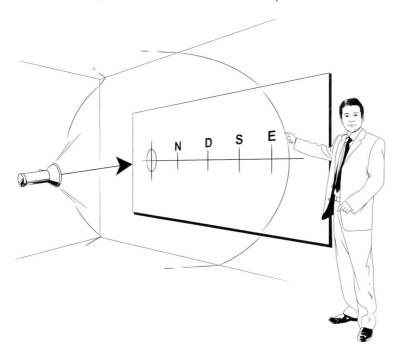

FIGURE 3.1 Demonstration set-up for gaining assessments of noticeable, distinct, strong and emphatic illumination differences.

created by controlling the distribution of illumination within a space. From Table 2.2 it can be seen that where the aim is to achieve a difference that is sufficient to be noticed, you can forget about 10 or 20 per cent differences. Unless a difference of at least 1.5:1 is provided, people will not notice the illumination to be anything different from uniform. To achieve differences that are likely to be described as 'distinct' or 'strong', it is necessary for the designer to be purposeful and deliberate in how they achieve such pronounced visual effects. Illumination distributions will have to be carefully controlled and, preferably, surrounding reflectances kept low. An 'emphatic' difference is quite difficult to achieve other than in a theatre or similar setting, and as was noted towards the end of Chapter 2, raising the target illumination unavoidably raises the ambient illumination. Where the aim is to achieve high illuminance differences, target objects need to be small in relation to their surrounding space, or more specifically, to the room absorption of the surrounding space.

We will return to this last point, but before moving on, let it be repeated that making assessments of the appearance of illumination differences is a revealing exercise in observation. Actually doing it, and measuring one's own assessments of perceived difference, is instructive. Then following up with observation and measurement in real locations is enormously valuable. The meter tells you nothing useful until you have related its readings to your own experience. The data in Table 2.2 is typical, but a designer needs to be able to visualise these illuminance ratios. It is by having in mind the perceived effect of illuminance ratios that a designer is able to specify values that reflect observation-based experience.

Target/ambient illuminance ratios

While the perceived adequacy of illumination (PAI) criterion is concerned with ensuring adequate inter-reflected flux (MRSE) within a space, the *illumination hierarchy* criterion is concerned with how the direct flux from the luminaires may be distributed to create an ordered pattern of illumination that supports selected lighting design objectives, which may range from directing attention to the functional activities of the space to creating aesthetic or artistic effects. For all of this, we make use of the *target/ambient illuminance ratio, TAIR,* where target illuminance is the sum of direct and indirect components, and TAIR relates target illuminance to the ambient illumination level. The designer selects target surfaces and designates values according to the level of perceived difference of illumination brightness to be achieved both between room surfaces, and between objects and the surroundings against which they are seen. As the point has been made that illumination is not visible until it has undergone its first reflection, it may be wondered why we are now dealing with incident target illumination, which comprises both direct and indirect illumination. The answer is that as both components undergo reflection at the same surface, it makes no difference whether we take the ratio of the incident or reflected values.

MRSE provides the measure of ambient illumination within a space, and except where there are obvious reasons to the contrary, it is reasonable to assume that the incident illumination on each target surface *tgt* will be the sum of direct illuminance and MRSE, so the total illuminance on a target surface:

$$E_{tgt} = E_{tgt(d)} + MRSE \qquad (3.1)$$

and the target/ambient illuminance ratio:

$$TAIR = E_{tgt} / MRSE \qquad (3.2)$$

The TAIR concept provides a basis for planning a distribution of direct flux from the luminaires that will achieve an envisioned illumination distribution within a space. It follows that for any chosen target surface, the direct illuminance:

$$E_{tgt(d)} = MRSE(TAIR - 1) \qquad (3.3)$$

Designing an illumination hierarchy involves designating *TAIR* values for selected surfaces or objects to signal noticeable, distinct, or strong perceived differences of illumination, again referring back to Table 2.2, and there really is no limit to the situations for which this procedure may be applied. A designer may choose to target a substantial proportion of the total room surface area, and examples of this would include lighting a mural covering a whole wall, or an architectural icon, or a library reading area, or perhaps, the horizontal work plane of an industrial assembly shop. Alternatively, the target area may be a single object that comprises a small proportion of the total surface area, such as a solitary sculpture, or a featured retail display, or the preacher in his pulpit; or it may comprise a number of even smaller items, such as display of coins, or individually lit items of glassware. Whatever the situation, the designer first needs to decide upon the *MRSE* level to achieve the required ambient illumination for the space, and then to decide upon the *TAIR* for each target surface for the differences of illumination brightness. This enables Formula 3.3 to be applied to draw up the distribution of direct target illuminance values.

This puts the designer in the position of being able to determine the distribution of direct light to be applied throughout the space in order to achieve the envisioned distribution of reflected light. The total indirect flux provided by first reflections from all surfaces receiving selective target lighting:

$$F_{ts(i)} = \sum E_{tgt(d)} A_{tgt} \rho_{tgt} \qquad (3.4)$$

Note that the suffix *tgt* indicates an individual target surface, and *ts* refers to all target surfaces within the space. This value of $F_{ts(i)}$ indicates the extent to which all of the selective target lighting will contribute towards the first reflected flux required to achieve the ambient illumination MRSE. The usefulness of this formula becomes apparent in the following section.

It may be noted in passing that, unlike MRSE, TAIR is not proposed as a suitable metric for lighting standards. TAIR is a tool that enables pursuit of chosen lighting design objectives, which may range from very simple through to distinctly complex in nature, and its application involves objectives that are beyond the scope of standards, whether advisory or mandatory.

Illumination hierarchy design procedure

Without wishing to give the impression that creative lighting design can be achieved by following a step-by-step procedure, the concepts previously described imply a sequence for logical decision making. The flowchart shown in Figure 3.2 should be referred to while following this procedure.

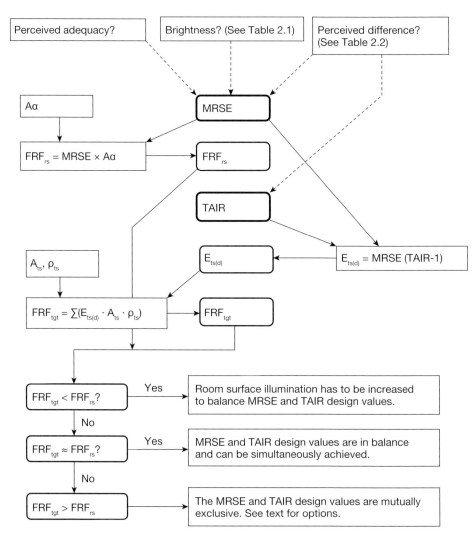

FIGURE 3.2 Flowchart for achieving mean room surface exitance, MRSE, and task/ambient illumination, TAIR, design values.

1   For a design location, consider a level of MRSE that would provide for an appropriate appearance of overall brightness or dimness. Codes or standards specified in task plane illuminance are unlikely to be helpful. Should there be a published MRSE value relevant to the location, it probably relates to the perceived adequacy of illumination (PAI) criterion and specifies the minimum value of MRSE to be provided. Consider whether a higher level to give a brighter appearance would be appropriate, referring to Table 2.1 for guidance, and taking into account the immediately previous brightness experience of a person entering this space. Consider whether it is to appear brighter or dimmer than the previous space, and if so, by how much, this time referring to Table 2.2 for guidance. Where no minimum levels are specified, designing for an appearance of dimness becomes an option providing safety concerns are kept in mind.

2   Decide upon the design value of MRSE, this being the overall density of inter-reflected flux to be provided within the volume of the space, and enter this value into the Illumination Hierarchy spreadsheet (see Box 3.1, and use your own downloaded copy of the spreadsheet).

3   Estimate the area and reflectance value for each significant surface S within the room, making sure to include any surfaces or objects that you might decide to highlight with selective lighting, and enter these onto the spreadsheet. The spreadsheet calculates the room absorption value, $A_{\alpha(rs)}$, and the total first reflected flux, FRF_{rs}, required to provide the MRSE value.

4   Consider the illumination hierarchy that the light distribution is to create in this space. Think about which objects or surface areas you want to highlight with selective lighting, and by how much. You will provide direct light onto these target surfaces, while surrounding areas will be lit mainly, or perhaps entirely, by reflected light.

5   Enter your design value of TAIR for each target area, taking account of how the appearance of the selected objects or surfaces will be affected by localised direct illumination. This listing of TAIR in Column 5 of the spreadsheet becomes the record of your illumination hierarchy for the space.

6   The spreadsheet completes the calculations, giving the first reflected flux to be provided by light reflected from the targets, FRF_{ts}, and the difference between this value and the total FRF required to provide the MRSE value, $FRF_{rs} - FRF_{ts}$.

Then:

•   If the first reflected flux from the targets is less than the total first reflected flux required, that is to say, if $FRF_{ts} < FRF_{rs}$, then in addition to the light directed onto the target areas, the surrounding room surfaces will need some direct illumination to make up for the difference, $FRF_{rs} - FRF_{ts}$. This is needed to ensure that the MRSE design value will be achieved. The direct illumination onto the room surfaces does not need to be applied uniformly, and often the most effective way will be to spread light over large, high-reflectance surrounding surfaces such as ceiling and walls. Concentrating this light onto small areas may cause them to compete visually with the target areas, as has been discussed in Chapter 2. There is plenty of scope for ingenuity in devising ways of raising the overall illumination brightness without detracting from the selected targets.

- If $FRF_{ts} \approx FRF_{rs}$, the target illumination alone will provide for the design values for both MRSE and TAIR. This is because reflected light from the target surfaces will both provide the design level of ambient illumination and achieve the intended balance of target/ambient levels. A serendipitous outcome.

- If $FRF_{ts} > FRF_{rs}$, the proposed balance of MRSE and TAIR values cannot be achieved in this situation. The reason is that if the direct target illuminance is applied, the reflected flux will raise MRSE above the design level, and reduce TAIR values below the design levels. Usually the most effective remedial action will be to reduce the total target area, such as by concentrating the objects to receive direct light into more restricted areas. Otherwise, it will be necessary to reduce either, or both, ρ_{ts} and ρ_{rs}, but unfortunately, lighting designers seldom have much influence over reflectance values. A compromise may be inevitable, but at least the outcome will not come as an unwelcome surprise.

Example: a banking premises

Box 3.1 shows a worksheet from the Illumination Hierarchy spreadsheet, and again, readers are strongly recommended to experience the use of these design tools. Room surface data have been entered for a banking premises, so take a moment to familiarise yourself with the location.

A bright and business-like appearance is wanted, and a MRSE level of 200 lm/m² is proposed. This value has been entered, and as previously, data shown in red are input by the user and all other values are calculated automatically. Column 4 gives the computed room absorption values, and the bottom line shows that 39,096 lumens of first reflected flux from the room surfaces is required to provide the MRSE level. Next the designer enters a TAIR value for selected target surfaces. This is the vital component of this stage of the design process, and Column 5 forms the statement of the designer's initial intent for illumination hierarchy. At the bottom of the final column it is shown that 20,899 lm of the required FRF will be provided from the target surfaces, so that the difference of 18,197 lm will need to be made up by applying additional direct light onto room surfaces.

This is the information that the designer needs to determine the balance of direct and indirect illumination. Various options for providing the deficit *FRF* may come to mind, but a simple and efficient solution would be uplighting. The required direct ceiling illuminance is:

$$E_{clg(d)} = FRF_{clg} / (A_{clg} \cdot \rho_{clg})$$
$$= 18197 / (113.3 \times 0.75) = 214 \text{ lux}$$

This direct illuminance added to the MRSE value of 200 lm/m² would give a total ceiling illuminance E_{clg} of 414 lux, giving a TAIR value of just over two. Table 2.2 indicates that this would correspond to a perceived difference that would appear somewhere between noticeable and distinct, and so would create a visible effect that might compete with the planned distribution of TAIR values. This effect could be reduced by applying less illumination onto the ceiling and making up for the deficiency by adding some direct light onto other surfaces, particularly the walls.

It is at this point that the attraction of using the spreadsheet becomes evident. By treating selected room surfaces as targets, alternative strategies may be readily examined. As the wall surfaces have lower reflectance values than the ceiling, it will take more direct

---

BOX 3.1

ILLUMINATION HIERARCHY SPREADSHEET

Date: 140119

Project Name: Banking Hall   Initial design

MRSE   200 lm/m^2

Room Surface	As m^2	ρs	Aαs	TAIR	$E_{tgt(d)}$ lx	FRF$_{tgt}$ lm
Ceiling	113.3	0.75	28.3	1	0	0
Wall 1	19.8	0.65	6.9	1	0	0
Mural, wall 1	29.7	0.35	19.3	3	400	4158
Wall 2	40.3	0.65	14.1	1	0	0
Wall 3	24.8	0.65	8.6	1	0	0
Blinds, wall 3	24.8	0.8	4.9	1	0	0
Wall 4	28.2	0.65	9.8	1	0	0
Blinds, wall 4	12.1	0.8	2.4	1	0	0
Floor, public	51	0.25	38.2	1.5	100	1275
Floor, private	45.3	0.15	38.5	3	400	2718
Counter top	17	0.55	7.6	5	800	7480
Counter front	21.4	0.3	14.9	3	400	2568
Display panels	3	0.5	1.5	10	1800	2700

		Aαrs	195 m^2	FRFts		20899 lm
		FRFrs	39096 lm	FRFrs – FRFts =		18197 lm

Symbols

As, Aαs	area of surface S, room absorption of S (m^2)
E	illuminance (lux)
FRF	first reflected flux (lm)
MRSE	mean room surface exitance (lm/m^2)
ρ, α	reflectance, absorptance
s, rs	individual surface, all room surfaces
TAIR	target/ambient illuminance ratio
tgt, ts	individual target surface, all target surfaces

lumens to bring the FRF_{rs} value up to the required level, but the light-coloured blinds in walls 3 and 4 could receive selective wallwashing, and this might create an attractive appearance. However, the effectiveness of this solution would depend upon the staff pulling down the blinds during hours of darkness. It would be necessary to enquire whether this could be relied upon, and after all, this is the way that lighting design happens. It is part of the reason why no two designers would come up with identical schemes.

Box 3.2 shows a design proposal. The TAIR values in Column 5 have been adjusted to provide various levels of unnoticeable, noticeable, distinct and strong perceived

---

BOX 3.2

ILLUMINATION HIERARCHY SPREADSHEET

Date: 140119

Project Name: Banking Hall   Final design proposal

MRSE   200 lm/m²

Room Surface	As m²	ρs	Aαs	TAIR	$E_{tgt(d)}$ lx	FRF_{tgt} lm
Ceiling	113.3	0.75	28.3	1.25	50	4248
Wall 1	19.8	0.65	6.9	1.25	50	643
Mural, wall 1	29.7	0.35	19.3	4	600	6237
Wall 2	40.3	0.65	14.1	1	0	0
Wall 3	24.8	0.65	8.6	1.25	50	806
Blinds, wall 3	24.8	0.8	4.9	2.5	300	5952
Wall 4	28.2	0.65	9.8	1.25	50	916.5
Blinds, wall 4	12.1	0.8	2.4	2.5	300	2904
Floor, public	51	0.25	38.2	1.5	100	1275
Floor, private	45.3	0.15	38.5	3	400	2718
Counter top	17	0.55	7.6	5	800	7480
Counter front	21.4	0.3	14.9	3	400	2568
Display panels	3	0.5	1.5	10	1800	2700
		Aαrs	195 m²	FRFts		38449 lm
		FRFrs	39096 lm	FRFrs – FRFts =		647 lm

Symbols

As, Aαs	area of surface S, room absorption of S (m²)
E	illuminance (lux)
FRF	first reflected flux (lm)
MRSE	mean room surface exitance (lm/m²)
ρ, α	reflectance, absorptance
s, rs	individual surface, all room surfaces
TAIR	target/ambient illuminance ratio
tgt, ts	individual target surface, all target surfaces

differences, and by adding more target surfaces in this way, the $FRF_{rs} - FRF_{ts}$ difference has been reduced to a negligible value. This means that the first reflected flux from the targets will provide the required 200 lm/m² of mean room surface exitance, and with the exception of the blinds, the visible effect of this additional illumination will not be bright enough to be noticed. In this way, the original design intent will be maintained. It can be seen not all surfaces are to receive direct light.

Column 6 shows the direct illuminance to be provided onto each target surface. All that is left now is to apply some straightforward illumination engineering, and procedures for determining luminaire layouts to distribute direct flux to achieve specific illuminance values are explained in Chapter 6.

References

Lynes, J.A. (1987). Patterns of light and shade. *Lighting in Australia*, 7(4): 16–20.
Waldram, J.M. (1954). Studies in interior lighting. *Transactions of the Illuminating Engineering Society (London)*; 19: 95–133.

4

SPECTRAL ILLUMINATION DISTRIBUTIONS

Chapter summary

Various ways in which human perception of a lit space is influenced by the spectral power distribution (SPD) of illumination are reviewed. Distinction is made between assessment of light for visibility and for brightness, and alternative response functions for indoor spaces are examined. The effects of SPD upon the perception of illumination colour (colour appearance) and coloured materials (colour rendering) are examined, along with various proposals for identifying how both SPD and illumination level influence the appearance of lit spaces. These include perceived attributes of illumination, such as the whiteness, naturalness and colourfulness of illumination, as well as some non-visual effects. It is concluded that people have different daytime and night time expectations and needs for lighting.

Luminous sensitivity functions

Before 1924, the only way of measuring light was to make comparisons with a familiar light source, which led to metrics such as the candle power and the foot candle, but in that year the CIE (International Commission on Illumination) introduced the $V(\lambda)$ luminous sensitivity function which defines the relative visual response, V, as a function of the wavelength of radiant power, λ, as shown in Figure 4.1. This was a significant breakthrough that required innovative research, and it enabled luminous flux, F, to be defined in terms of lumens from a measurement of spectral power distribution:

$$F = 683\Sigma P(\lambda)V(\lambda)\Delta_\lambda \qquad (4.1)$$

where:

P(λ) = spectral power, in watts, of the source at the wavelength λ

V(λ) = photopic luminous efficiency function value at λ

Δ_λ = interval over which the values of spectral power were measured

It can be seen from Figure 4.1 that V(λ) has its maximum value of 1.0 at 555nm, and so the luminous efficiency of radiant flux at this wavelength is equal to the value of the constant in Formula 4.1, 683 lm/W. At 610nm, where the value of V(λ) is approximately 0.5, the luminous efficiency reduces to half that value.

So by defining the V(λ) function, the CIE made it possible for the output of a light source to be specified in terms of the lumen, while at the same time enabling light itself to be defined in terms of radiant power within the waveband 380–780 nanometres (nm). To this day, lighting standards and recommended practice documents, as well as the calibration of all light meters, are based on V(λ), and in fact, it continues to be quite appropriate for measuring illumination in situations where photopically-adapted viewers are fixating upon visual tasks. Examples range from a library reading room to a hospital operating theatre, and for these, as well as for most task-based applications in between, this luminous sensitivity function continues to serve us well. There is, however, more to human response to light than this, and for designers to be able to apply lighting knowingly and effectively in the range of situations encountered in general lighting practice, we could benefit from metrics that take account of a wider range of human interactions with radiant flux.

Formula 4.1 assumes a human observer operating within the range of photopic vision, and this means that error is incurred whenever V(λ) is applied for mesopic or scotopic conditions. Also, the researchers who established the V(λ) function had their subjects observing a quite small luminous patch that subtended just 2 degrees at the eye, so that it

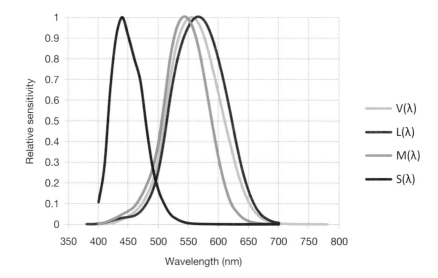

FIGURE 4.1 Relative sensitivity functions for V(λ), and the three cone types; long-, medium- and short-wavelength; L(λ), M(λ) and S(λ). It can be seen how closely V(λ) represents the responses of the L and M cones, and ignores the S cone response.

was illuminating only the foveal regions of the subjects' retinas. The photoreceptors in these central regions are only long- and medium-wavelength responsive cones, which are often (but inaccurately) referred to as the red and green cones, and their luminous sensitivity functions are shown in Figure 4.1 as L(λ) and M(λ) respectively. It should be noted how similar are the responses of these two cones, particularly when it is borne in mind that it is the difference in response of this pair of two cone types that enables colour discrimination on the red–green axis, and also, how closely similar they are to V(λ). The responses of the short-wavelength (blue) cones, shown as the S(λ) function, as well as all of the rods, are simply not taken into account by the V(λ) function.

For a photopically-adapted viewer, the S(λ) function does not affect acuity for a fixated task, but it does affect assessments of the brightness of the surrounding field, and this occurs to an extent that changes with field luminance. The Bezold-Brücke hue shift describes the effect of perceived colour differences on the blue–yellow axis increasing relative to those on the red–green axis with increasing luminance, and this affects brightness assessments. Rea *et al.* (2011) have proposed a luminous sensitivity function for brightness:

$$B(\lambda) = V(\lambda) + g.S(\lambda)$$

(4.2)

where the value of g is related to field luminance. In this way, a variable allowance for the response of the short-wavelength cones can be added to the long- and medium-wavelength cones dominated V(λ), and Mark Rea has tentatively suggested that for the range of luminous environments discussed in this book, for which 10 <MRSE <1000 lm/m^2, a g value of 3.0 would be appropriate. The resulting luminous sensitivity function, indicated as $V_{B3}(\lambda)$, is shown in Figure 4.2. It is proposed that applying this function for predicting or measuring MRSE would give more reliable results, in terms of better matching metrics to assessments, than using conventional lumen-based metrics.

Meanwhile the CIE has given attention to other deficiencies of V(λ) by defining additional luminous sensitivity functions, the most notable being the V'(λ) function introduced in 1951, which defines the relative response of the rod photoreceptors, and so relates to scotopically-adapted vision (Figure 4.3). This function shows substantially greater sensitivity for shorter wavelength (blue) radiant flux, but while research scientists are able to recalculate luminous flux according to the viewing conditions, this does not happen in general lighting practice. The notion that the lumen output of a lamp might depend on the circumstances of its use is a complication that the lighting industry would not welcome, and so the 1924 V(λ) function persists. Until lighting practice comes to terms with this discrepancy, some level of mismatch between measured or predicted lighting performance and human response is inevitable. For designers, it becomes a matter of how we balance simplicity and convenience against actually providing what we have promised.

It may be noted that the visual field has to become distinctly dark, with adaptation luminance less than 0.001 cd/m^2, for vision to become entirely due to the rod photosensors. When this occurs, scotopic conditions prevail and the V'(λ) luminous sensitivity function applies, so that scotopic luminous flux:

$$F' = 1700\Sigma P(\lambda)V'(\lambda)\Delta_\lambda$$

(4.3)

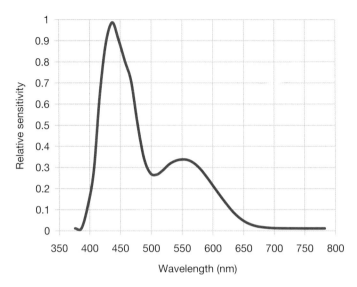

FIGURE 4.2 The $V_{B3}(\lambda)$ spectral sensitivity of brightness function for daytime light levels, where the contribution of the S cones relative to $V(\lambda)$ is high (g = 3). After Rea (2013).

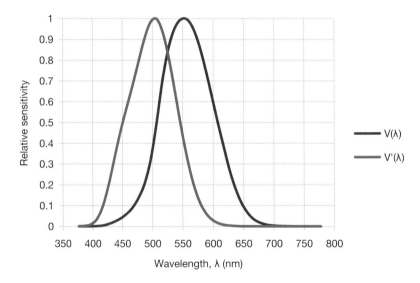

FIGURE 4.3 The $V(\lambda)$ and $V'(\lambda)$ relative luminous efficiency functions relate to photopic and scotopic adaptation respectively.

In this way, while the photopic luminous flux, F, for a given source is determined by application of Formula 4.1, its scotopic lumens, F', could be determined by application of Formula 4.3. Note the increased value of the constant in this formula to reflect the high sensitivity of dark-adapted rods. It follows that if the value of F'/F, referred to as the S/P (scotopic/photopic) ratio, is high, then at low light levels, where the rods are active, the visual response will be underrated. Sources rich at shorter wavelengths, such as metal halide lamps, will, for the same lumens, generate stronger visual responses than lamps rich at longer wavelengths, such as sodium lamps.

Some other visual and non-visual responses

While it would seem quite straightforward that F' should be used as the measure for luminous flux for scotopic conditions, these conditions are in fact so dim that nobody actually provides illumination to achieve them. Lighting practice for outdoor spaces, such as car parks, roadways and airport runways, aims to provide conditions in the mesopic range, which extends from 0.001 cd/m^2 up to the lower limit of the photopic range, at 3 cd/m^2. Within this substantial adaptation luminance range, spectral sensitivity undergoes transition between scotopic and photopic adaptation, and where we are concerned with brightness assessments, this means transition between the very dissimilar $V'(\lambda)$ and $V_{B3}(\lambda)$ functions, which makes accurate assessment of the likely visual response problematic (Rea, 2013). This is a real issue for providing illumination at outdoor lighting levels.

For indoor lighting at photopic levels, there are some different issues that concern researchers. It has been established that, at the same luminance levels, pupil size is smaller for higher S/P illumination, and this led to the assumption that pupil size is determined by the response of the rod photoreceptors, even at photopic levels. Berman *et al.* (1993) conducted a series of laboratory studies for tasks close to the visual threshold (the point at which there is a 50/50 probability of accurate detection) and showed that performance was better for higher S/P sources. It might seem odd that reduced pupil size, which must reduce the amount of light reaching the retina, should give increased performance, but the explanation offered was that reducing the lens aperture would improve the quality of the retinal image. As with a camera, smaller lens aperture gives increased depth of field, which is an advantage for anyone whose refractive correction is less than perfect. It also occurs that rays passing through the peripheral zones of the eye's lens tend to undergo aberrations, as the lens of the eye is, in fact, of no more than moderate optical quality, so that reducing observers' pupil sizes is likely to cause them to experience improved image resolution. It was claimed that these advantages would more than compensate for the reduced retinal illuminance.

Application of the S/P findings to lighting practice has recently been the subject of both research and debate. The notion that visual performance could be maintained at lower illuminance levels offers opportunities for significant energy savings, and this certainly has aroused interest, but it has been pointed out that the higher performance demonstrated for threshold visual tasks would be unlikely to apply for the much more usual condition of suprathreshold tasks. General lighting practice aims to ensure that tasks are performed with high rates of accuracy, meaning that they are to be illuminated to well above their threshold levels, so that advantages that may occur in an experiment where the probability of error is high probably would not occur in practical situations (Boyce, 2003). A recent field study by Wei *et al.* (2014) of office workers found not only that any advantages attributable to high S/P sources were too small to be worthwhile, but also that the people working in those conditions disliked the high S/P lighting. Among the research community there now seems to be a lack of interest in pursuing this topic, but that has not stopped some unscrupulous suppliers from making claims that are exaggerated, and even downright false, for high S/P lamps. It may be noted in passing that since the original investigations, researchers have become aware that pupil size response is more complex than simply responding to the level of rod cells stimulation, and seems to involve the recently discovered ipRGC response (see following paragraph).

Humans exhibit various non-visual responses to light, and the most important, at least from our point of view, is the circadian response, being the 24-hour cycle that we experience along with most living things on this planet. With the onset of circadian night, a hormone named melatonin is released from the pineal gland into the bloodstream, and this is associated with the sleep/wake cycle that is said to be regulated by a hypothetical biological clock that each one of us carries inside us. Researchers had noted that the melatonin response to light exposure displays a spectral sensitivity that does not match that of any of the retinal photoreceptors, but it was not until 2002 that the mystery was solved. The answer lies in the complex pattern of connections within the retina that link the photoreceptors to the optic nerve for communication to the brain. Retinal ganglion cells were known to play major roles in this process, but what had not been suspected was that some of these cells actually contain a photopigment, which has been named melanopsin, and the light response of these intrinsically photosensitive retinal ganglion cells (ipRGCs) connects not to the visual cortex, but to the endocrine gland, and on to the pineal gland. The peak sensitivity of these cells due to the melanopsin photopigment occurs at 460 nm, which is substantially shorter than the peak responses of any of the retinal photocells.

Rea (2013) has proposed a spectral sensitivity function, $V_C(\lambda)$, for the human circadian response, which is shown in Figure 4.4. This is rather different from the other functions

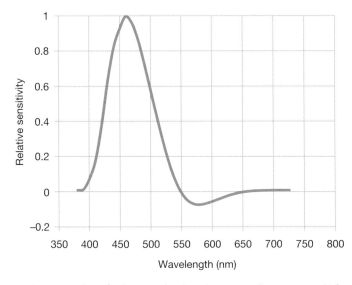

FIGURE 4.4 Rea's proposed $V_C(\lambda)$ function for the relative circadian response (After Rea, 2013).

discussed so far in that it is not the response of a cell, but of a system. A large part of the response is additive, meaning that light at these wavelengths will have the effect of dispersing melatonin from the blood, and part is subadditive, which means that for a broad-spectrum source, energy at these wavelengths will have a negative effect, but if the total sum for the whole spectrum is negative, the response should be assumed to be zero.

Taking account of this function calls for a quite different way of thinking about the impact of light exposure. Before the invention of electric lighting, illumination after sunset was either absent, or it was of low intensity and biased toward longer wavelengths, so that circadian cycles were largely undisturbed by after-dusk light exposure. While we all applaud the benefits of electric lighting, a consequence has been a substantial growth in nocturnal light exposure, and while many find this lifestyle choice attractive, health studies of people who engage in it over long periods, such as shift workers and airline staff, are a cause for concern. There is reason to suppose that daytime exposure to illumination that scores highly on the circadian spectral sensitivity function, followed by night time exposure to reduced levels of low scoring illumination, would be conducive to long-term health.

While these human responses to light represent concerns that lighting designers can never ignore, there are two principal concerns for the spectral distribution of illumination that must always be at the forefront of a lighting designer's mind. These are how the colour appearance of the illumination relates to the design concept of the space, and how the colours of illuminated objects within the space will be rendered by the illumination.

Colour appearance of illumination

It is common experience that some materials can be heated to the point where they become incandescent, starting from a dull red, increasing with temperature through bright crimson to brilliant white-hot. Most materials would melt or evaporate if the temperature was to be further increased, but the theoretical 'black-body' does not have this limitation and its temperature can be raised until it becomes 'blue-hot'.

When lamp makers discovered how to step beyond the restrictions of producing light by incandescence, that opened up opportunities to produce light with different spectra, including light that was not far removed from white but which was distinctly different from the warm, yellowish light emitted by a hot metal filament. In fact, it became possible to produce light that matched the appearance of different phases of daylight illumination, but this raised the question of how to describe these variation of 'white' light in a way that would make sense to people choosing, or specifying, these new-fangled discharge and fluorescent lamps.

The answer they came up with was to define the colour appearance of all types of nominally 'white' light sources in terms of correlated colour temperature (CCT), this being the temperature of a black-body, specified in degrees Kelvin, that most closely matched the appearance of the source in question. In Figure 4.5, the 'black-body locus' defines the change in chromaticity of emitted light from the black-body as its temperature is varied, and it can be seen that this corresponds to the commonly experienced change of colour of emitted light when materials are heated. The invention of the halogen cycle enabled

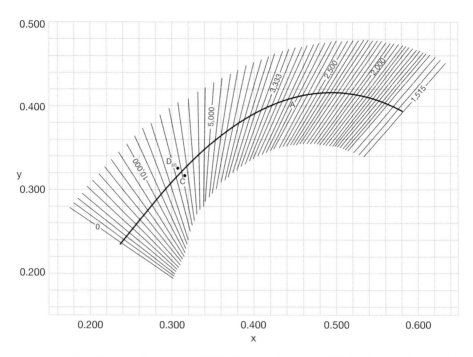

FIGURE 4.5 The black-body locus (solid line) plotted on the CIE 1931 (x,y) chromaticity chart with intersecting lines of constant correlated colour temperature indicated in degrees Kelvin. Also shown are the chromaticity coordinates of CIE Standard Illuminants, A, C, and D65 (from IESNA 2000).

incandescent filaments to be maintained at temperatures of up 3300K, and CCT described the appearance of the emitted light quite reliably. However, the real need for being able to indicate the colour appearance of illumination was the developing market for fluorescent lamps, where spectral distribution has nothing to do with temperature. There was demand for light sources that could provide 'white hot', and even 'blue-hot', illumination colours, as well as the colours of daylight illumination, and fluorescent lamps made all of this possible. Figure 4.6 shows CCT values for some familiar lamp types related to colour appearance. The confusing ways in which the CCT scale associates low colour temperatures with warm colour appearance and high colour temperatures with cool colour appearance, and that intervals on this scale are quite out of step with perceived differences, are both neatly overcome by the reciprocal mega Kelvin scale (MK^{-1}). While lamp makers have recognised the usefulness of this scale, it has not come into general use and, in any case, it has the disadvantage that it associates the chromaticity of a black-body with whiteness, and this has had unfortunate consequences that have been shown up by recent research.

Rea and Freyssinier (2013) have reported a study in which subjects described the appearance of different lighting chromaticities, and it was found that there is an extended range of chromaticities that may appear 'white', or with minimum perceived 'tint', and importantly, these chromaticities do not follow the line of the black-body locus. Figure 4.7 shows a section of the black-body locus crossed by lines of constant colour

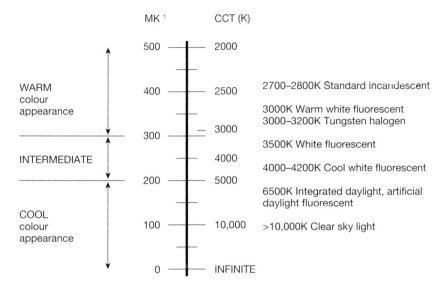

FIGURE 4.6 The reciprocal mega Kelvin scale (MK⁻¹) compared with the Kelvin (K) scale, and with typical assessments of colour appearance and CCTs of some familiar light sources.

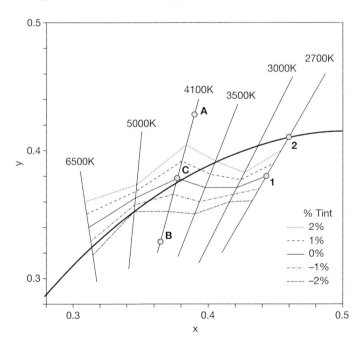

FIGURE 4.7 Contours of perceived level of tint. The solid line is the black-body locus plotted on the CIE 1931 chromaticity chart. The line of 0% tint is the contour of source chromaticities perceived to have minimum tint at that colour temperature, and these are referred to as 'white' sources, with other lines showing increasing levels of perceived tint. See text for more explanation (from Rea, 2013).

temperature (see Figure 4.5), and superimposed over these are lines of perceived level of tint. The 0% line is the experimentally-derived contour of 'white' sources. This does not mean that source chromaticities on this contour appear identical, but rather that at a given colour temperature, any source chromaticity on this contour is perceived to be with minimum tint. While sources A, B, and C all have the same colour temperature of 4100K, they will be perceived quite differently. In fact, source C will appear more similar to source 1 than to either A or B, as both C and 1 appear to be with minimum tint. Departures above (+ive) or below (-ive) this contour incur increasing perceived tint, where for different points along this contour, positive tint may appear slightly yellow, chartreuse or green, and negative may appear slightly pink, purple or blue (Rea, 2013). It should be noted that this 'white' source locus departs significantly from the black-body contour, being above it for CCTs above 4000K, and below it for CCTs below 4000K.

Seen in this way, it becomes obvious why conventional light sources around 4000K have been described as 'white', and lower colour temperature light sources are perceived to be yellowish-white and are said to appear 'warm', and higher colour temperature sources are perceived to be bluish-white and are said to appear 'cool'. The notion of the 'black-body' being the standard reference source is ingrained to the point that as the lighting industry has developed newer technologies, such as compact fluorescent lamps and now LED sources, repeatedly their aim is to match the characteristics of traditional sources. At the time of writing, examples are occurring of lighting companies advertising new LED sources by claiming that the illumination is indistinguishable from halogen lighting. There is, however, at least one LED manufacturer that is promoting its product as departing from the black-body locus, but even so, it may be some while before we have opportunities to experience tint-free 'white' illumination of different colour temperatures in spaces that enable us to properly assess their appearance.

Illuminance and illumination colour preference

It was way back in 1941 that A.A. Kruithof, a lamp development engineer with Philips Lighting in the Netherlands, wrote an article describing the fluorescent lamp. This lamp had been introduced in the USA only three years earlier, and despite the turmoil of the Second World War, it was finding its way into Europe. Among the many unfamiliar aspects of this new technology that Kruithof described was that it would be possible to select the CCT of lighting. This had not been possible previously, and to provide guidance on how to do this, he included the diagram reproduced in Figure 4.8. This figure is possibly the most reproduced diagram in the history of lighting. The white zone indicates acceptable combinations of illuminance and CCT, and within the lower shaded zone, which includes combinations of low illuminance and high CCT, Kruithof described the effect as 'cold and harsh', while in the upper shaded zone, which includes combinations of high illuminance and low CCT, he described the effect as 'unnatural' (Kruithof 1941).

The article gives little information on how this diagram was derived, but Kruithof has told the author that it was a 'pilot study' based entirely on the observations by himself and his assistant. For low colour temperatures, incandescent lamps were switched from series to parallel, but as the halogen lamp had not been invented, those conditions would have

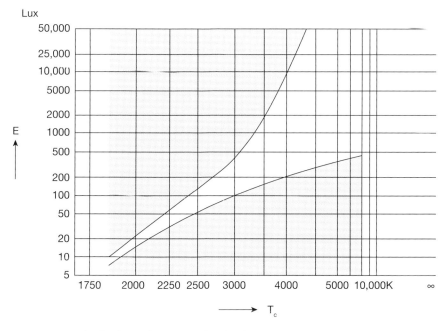

FIGURE 4.8 Kruithof's chart relating correlated colour temperature (T_C) and illuminance (E) to colour appearance. The white zone is described as 'preferred', while the lower shaded zone appears 'cold and harsh' and the upper zone appears 'unnatural' (from Kruithof, 1941).

been limited to 2800K. For higher CCTs, they used some 'special fluorescent lamps' that were currently under development, but even with the resources of the Philips research laboratories at that time, the range of phosphors available would have been restricting. For some parts of the diagram, Kruithof relied on a common sense approach. It is obvious that outdoor daylight with a CCT of 5000K at an illuminance of 50,000 lux is very acceptable, so he extrapolated to that point. It was in this way that the diagram of the 'Kruithof effect' was put together.

Since that time, several researchers have sought to apply scientific method to defining a sound basis for this phenomenon, but this has proved an elusive goal. However, the 'Kruithof effect' lives on. Lighting designers continue to refer to it with reverence, and perhaps more convincingly, you are unlikely to find opportunities to carry out observations of lighting installation that occur in the shaded areas of the diagram. You will find that the higher lighting levels provided in commercial and industrial locations, whether by fluorescent or high intensity discharge lamps, tend to make use of CCTs corresponding to the intermediate or cool ranges shown in Figure 4.6. Even where CCTs higher than 5000K are used, if the illuminance also is high (say more than 1500 lux), the effect is more inclined towards a bright and colourful appearance reminiscent of daylight, rather than a noticeably 'cool' effect. Conversely, where lighting is deliberately dim, the low CCTs of incandescent lamps, or even candles, are likely to be the chosen light sources. If you practise observation coupled with measurement, you are likely to find ample confirmation of the Kruithof effect.

Illumination colour and 'flow' of light

There is an interesting dimension of colour contrast that has been routinely exploited by stage lighting designers, and which has the potential to be influential in architectural lighting design. People are sometimes surprised by the appearance of colour photographs taken outdoors in sunny conditions. Areas in sunlight appear to have a yellow cast, and particularly for snow scenes, shadows appear noticeably blue. While our visual response tends to obscure this naturally occurring colour difference, if you look for it you can see it, and many artists, particularly the impressionists, have recorded their observations of this 'sun and sky' lighting effect.

Stanley McCandless incorporated the effect into his method for stage lighting (McCandless 1958). An essential feature of his approach is that all objects on stage are to be illuminated from opposite sides, with the light from one side having lower CCT to give a sunlight effect, and the light from the other side having higher CCT, perhaps of lower intensity, to give a skylight effect. In this way, a distinct and coherent 'flow' of light is achieved without strong shadows being cast. This means that an actor can remain clearly visible while having his face in the shadow.

When you are aware of this 'sun and sky' lighting effect, it is surprising how often you can find examples of it in retail display lighting. Car showrooms can achieve very effective displays by flooding the space with diffuse light using relatively efficient 'daylight' lamps which might have a CCT of more than 5000K, while providing highlighting from spotlights having CCT close to 3000K. Clothing stores often use lower CCT spotlights to strongly highlight selected items that are arranged as vertical eye-catching displays, while relying on the cooler appearance of general fluorescent lighting to reveal the daylight colours of the merchandise that the customers handle. Blue is a frequently used colour for the internal surfaces of display cabinets that have internal spotlights, and of course, it gives the sky effect to the shadows. Everybody sees 'flow' of light effects of this sort, but it takes a lighting designer to observe the visual effect and to understand how it can be provided.

Colour rendering of illumination

Among the more spectacular developments within the lighting industry during the past half century has been progressive improvement in colour rendering, being the influence that lighting has on the perceived colours of objects and materials. In fact, for most everyday lighting applications, colour rendering really has ceased to be a problem. Users have a choice of light sources that are quite satisfactory for industrial and office lighting applications, as well as for general lighting for retail, recreational, and social activities. It has not always been so, and when the Colour Rendering Index (usually abbreviated to CRI, but note also the use of scientific symbol R_a below) was introduced in 1965, it was a useful tool for sorting out the good, the indifferent and the plain ugly.

CRI continues to appear in codes, standards and specifications, where statements such as 'CRI shall be not less than 85' is a simple formula for avoiding lamp types that would cause unsatisfactory user responses. However, for the applications where colour rendering is an important factor, CRI fails to provide reliable guidance. Art gallery and museum directors have learned the hard way that simply specifying a high CRI value does not ensure excellent, or even acceptable, appearance of displays.

There have been several proposals over the years to make CRI more useful, or to replace it with something better. The following sections review some of these proposals and offers guidance on coming to terms with colour rendering.

The CIE Colour Rendering Index

The International Commission on Illumination (CIE) defines colour rendering as the 'effect of an illuminant on the colour appearance of objects by conscious or subconscious comparison with their colour appearance under a reference illuminant' (CIE, 1987).

The supposition here is that the observer is fully adapted to the same lighting that illuminates the objects, and that the colour appearance of the objects would be natural, and therefore optimal, if the lighting was provided by a reference source. The concept of a reference source is central to any discussion of colour rendering as it provides the basis for the comparison that is contained in the definition. It is an inherent assumption that the perceived colours of objects lit by the appropriate reference source would appear entirely acceptable, and that any departure from this appearance would be detrimental.

As the brightness and the colour of the ambient illumination in our environment changes, the response of our visual system adapts to the ambient condition. CRI assumes photopic adaptation and makes no adjustment for brightness, while the observer's state of chromatic adaptation is assumed to be determined by the chromaticity of the actual light source. The corresponding reference source is accorded a colour temperature that matches the correlated colour temperature (CCT) of the light source. For CCTs less than 5000K the reference source is the black-body, and for 5000K and above it is a CIE standard daylight distribution defined by its CCT. Getting these assumptions in mind is essential for understanding CRI.

The CRI values for a test source are determined by the Test Colour Method (CIE, 1994). Fourteen test colour samples (TCS), listed in Table 4.1, are defined by individual spectral reflectance curves. For each TCS, u,v chromaticity coordinates on the 1960 UCS (Uniform Chromaticity Scale) chart are calculated for both the test source and its reference source, and a colour adaptation transform is applied to allow for chromatic adaptation differences between the two sources. After that, colour differences in UCS space are calculated for each TCS under both sources. Each difference is defined by a vector that specifies the colour shift for viewing the TCS alternatively under the reference source and under the test source, allowing for adaptation to each source. The magnitude of each vector ΔE_i enables the Special Colour Rendering Index R_i for each TCS to be calculated:

$$R_i = 100 - 4.6 \, \Delta E_i \tag{4.4}$$

From only the first eight TCS values, the General Colour Rendering Index R_a is calculated:

$$R_a = 1/8 \sum_{i=1}^{8} R_i \tag{4.5}$$

TABLE 4.1 The 14 CIE TCS (Test colour samples). TCS 1–8 comprise the original set of moderately saturated colours representing the whole hue circle, and these are the only samples used for determining CRI. The other six have been added for additional information, and comprise four saturated colours, TCS 9–12, and two surfaces of particular interest. Regrettably, details of colour shifts for these TCS are seldom made available

No.	Approximate Munsell notation	Colour appearance under daylight
1	7.5R 6/4	Light greyish red
2	5Y 6/4	Dark greyish yellow
3	5GY 6/8	Strong yellow green
4	2.5G 6/6	Moderate yellowish green
5	10BG 6/4	Light bluish green
6	5PB 6/8	Light blue
7	2.5P 6/8	Light violet
8	10P 6/8	Light reddish purple
9	4.5R 4/13	Strong red
10	5Y 8/10	Strong yellow
11	4.5G 5/8	Strong green
12	3PB 3/11	Strong blue
13	5YR 8/4	Light yellowish pink (human complexion)
14	5GY 4/4	Moderate olive green (leaf green)

This may seem complicated, but the CIE documentation includes a computer program that performs the task effortlessly. While this takes away the pain for the lamp manufacturer, it is necessary for us to understand what is being done so we can see how it might be done better. The program output for a standard Warm White halophosphate fluorescent lamp is shown in Figure 4.9.

There is plenty to ponder here. The lamp is, of course, an old-fashioned fluorescent lamp, and it is sobering to realise that when CRI was introduced in 1965, this was the standard lamp for general lighting practice. The program gives the x,y chromaticity coordinates, the CCT (T_c), and a measure of how far the chromaticity is off the black-body locus (dC). The CRI (R_a) is the average of R_i values for TCS 1–8, and it can be seen that these vary substantially. Referring to Table 4.1, colour shifts are relatively small for the yellow–green and violet TCSs, but become large in other zones. Then look at the strong colours, particularly the strong red, represented as TCS 9, for which the chromaticity shift is massive, but the value for this TCS was not, and still is not, taken into account by CRI. Human complexion (TCS 13) has a poor score, so it is no wonder that everybody was pleased to see the back of this lamp, and really, that has been the foremost achievement of CRI. Nobody would now dream of lighting an indoor space in which the appearance of people might be of some consequence with such an utterly dismal lamp.

```
File:    WARMWT.EMI
Path:    C:\DOCUME~1\CRI\
Title:   WarmWhite  fluor. lamp; No 5
```

Coords:
```
x=       0.4363
y=       0.4111
Tc=        3066 K
dC=      2.85e-03
```

Reference colours:
    CIE standard colours (1–14)
    Ra calculated based on the first eight colours

Special Rendering Indexes:
```
No. 1 =        42.1
No. 2 =        69.3
No. 3 =        89.8
No. 4 =        39.8
No. 5 =        41.6
No. 6 =        53.6
No. 7 =        66.2
No. 8 =        11.8
No. 9 =      −116.7
No. 10 =       29.9
No. 11 =       21.5
No. 12 =       24.4
No. 13 =       46.9
No. 14 =       94.0

Ra =           51.77
```

FIGURE 4.9   Output from CIE13 3W.exe computer program to calculate CRIs, for a Warm White halophosphate fluorescent lamp. While this is an old-fashioned lamp, this example illustrates well the colour rendering issues that CRI was devised to cope with.

Problems with CRI

Despite this level of success, CRI has several problems, some of which may be evident from the previous section. The CIE specifies 14 TCSs, and calculates CRI from just eight of them, ignoring the other six. The reason for this is that originally only TCS 1–8 were specified, and they are all medium saturation colours, but people had noted that lamps that might perform reasonably well for these colours could fail badly for rendering strong colours. Also, the appearances of human complexion and foliage have special significance as people have clear notions of how they should appear, and so it was decided that these too should be added. This led to the addition of six more TCSs, but then, rather than change CRI, it was decided that they should be listed separately to provide users with additional information. However, while the program output gives these values, most users are completely unaware of them. Manufacturers claim that people would be confused by the additional data, but nonetheless, it needs to be recognised that colour rendering is too complicated an issue to be adequately defined by a single number.

To illustrate this point, if data for the additional six TCSs were to be provided, what interpretation should be placed upon them? A low value of R_i indicates that the appearance of this TCS will be distinctly different under the test and reference sources, but no indication is given of the nature of that difference. For example, the negative R_i value noted for the strong red TCS might indicate that the test source shifts it towards yellow, giving an orange tint, or towards blue, giving a mauve tint. Alternatively, it might appear less saturated, giving a pink tint, or it might appear more saturated, appearing as a vivid red. Not only does CRI give no indication of which of these differences occurs, but it treats all of them as being equally detrimental. There is good evidence to indicate that, within reason, people like lamps that make their surroundings appear more colourful, that is to say, which cause increased saturation. This challenges the central notion that a reference source provides optimal colour rendering.

Another issue is that it has for some while been acknowledged that the 1960 UCS chart is far from uniform in its spacing of chromaticity values, and since then there have been several proposals for more uniform definitions of colour space. To change the colour space would affect CRI values, so this has not been done, with the result that CRI continues to be calculated using a procedure that is known to evaluate colour differences unequally.

There are other problems. The CRI scale causes confusion, some users supposing it to be a percentage scale, so the fact that some lamps are shown to have negative values comes as a surprise. Also, because CRI has been so widely used by specifiers, manufacturers have developed lamps to achieve high CRI values, so that they have incorporated the shortcomings of CRI into their new products. It has become increasingly apparent that this approach has led to lamps being promoted for good colour rendering but which have distinctly less than optimal performance. These shortcomings of CRI became clearly evident with the development of tri-phosphor fluorescent lamps in the 1970s, and they are now seen to be a substantial hindrance to progress by companies working on development of white LED sources. It is high time for changes to be made to CRI.

What is being done about CRI?

There has been no shortage of suggestions over the years, with past proposals for a Colour Discrimination Index, and even a Flattery Index. While these may have attracted attention at the times when they were proposed, the CIE has set up a Technical Committee to revise CRI and this project has gained support from the US National Institute for Science and Technology. It has led to the development of the Colour Quality Scale (CQS) (Davis and Ohno, 2004), which is a substantial revision of CRI and involves a new set of 15 test colour samples of high chromatic saturation spanning the entire hue circle, and it makes the switch to 1976 CIELAB colour space, which assesses different types of colour difference more closely to how they appear. Shifts of hue or shifts to lower saturation are treated as being equally detrimental, but shifts to higher saturation incur no penalty. A weighting is placed on CCT, so that for CCTs less than 3500K or more than 6500K, scores are modified by a scaled multiplication factor. This would have the effect, for example, of reducing the domestic incandescent lamp's rating from 100 to 97. The scale itself is modified to eliminate negative values, with the effect that all of the very poorly performing lamps will have ratings between 0 and 20.

The single rating indicator with a maximum value of 100 is retained, and the overall weighting of CQS between 20 and 100 is not too different from CRI, although ratings for some lamp types do undergo significant changes. In particular, it may be expected that lamps with multiple narrow waveband emissions, such as LED combinations, will achieve more favourable CQS ratings than the ratings they gain under CRI. Finally, to overcome the effect of averaging, by which a lamp may gain a moderately high score while one or two test colours show large colour differences, individual scores are calculated as root mean square (RMS) values.

The retention of a single scale indicator of colour rendering suits specifiers, who would continue to be able to prescribe a minimum value for a given application, and while it should reduce anomalies, it will not provide lighting designers with guidance on how the colour appearance of illuminated objects will be affected by the light source. So while CQS falls short of providing lighting designers with all the information they need, it does go a long way towards overcoming the anomalies incorporated into CRI. It is, however, important to appreciate that while CQS has been published and discussion invited, at the time of writing it had not been endorsed by the CIE.

What is the current state of knowledge on colour rendering?

Researchers in the colour science field have achieved remarkable success during the past decade, which has led to the development of colour appearance models (CAMs). Two scientists had independently developed models for predicting how a typical observer perceives colours in the environment, each taking account of a range of variables and known visual phenomena. Dr R.W.G. Hunt, with the Kodak Corporation in the UK, had spent a lifetime working on coloured images and Dr Y. Nayatani of Japan developed his model to address concerns in illumination engineering and colour rendering. In 1997, the two models were merged to produce a single Colour Appearance Model, CIECAM97s. This was taken up with enthusiasm in a range of industries where colour is a critical aspect of quality control, particularly where imaging is involved, and soon the CIE Technical Committee concerned had available a wealth of feedback gained from practical application. This led to CIECAM02, which was actually published in 2004, and is considered likely to remain unaltered for some while as it is believed to be as good a model as can be produced from current knowledge. For a review of CIECAM02, see Fairchild (2004).

The input data required to apply CIECAM02 to predict the colour appearance of an element in the field of view include colorimetric data for the object (stimulus) and the light source (adapting stimulus), the absolute luminance and colorimetric data of the proximal field, including the background and surround to the stimulus. The success of this model lies in the variety of potentially influential factors that may be taken into account. In Chapter 1 we noted how the colour appearance of an object can be affected by whether colours are perceived as related or unrelated, and in CIECAM02, the effect of surrounding surfaces upon the perception of surface colours is predictable. This is just one of a range of colour appearance phenomena that have been observed and reported over the years, and which have subsequently been researched and quantified, and now have been combined into a single comprehensive model.

The spectral power distribution of the light source is one of the input variables, and so aspects such as how bright and colourful a specific object will appear in a given setting could be examined for alternative lamps. In terms of applied scientific knowledge, this undoubtedly would be a leap forward. However, we cannot use CIECAM02 in the way that we use CRI, that is to say, we cannot use it to describe the colour properties of a lamp, as it has to be applied to a specific viewing situation. Perhaps this will become possible one day. The spectacular advances in computer visualisation software that have occurred during the past decade might enable us to model the effect of different light sources upon colour appearance of a real or simulated scene, but meanwhile, we need to think about what the information is that would be useful to us now.

What do we want to know about colour rendering?

When we get down to meeting actual needs for presenting coloured objects for critical examination and assessment, it becomes apparent that those who put such objects on display have learned a lot about people's preferences for colour appearance. For confirmation of this, you need look no further than your local supermarket. The fresh produce displays use different lamp types for the meat, fish, fruit and vegetables, as well as for the 'deli' displays, all of which have been chosen for how they render the colours of that particular type of merchandise, and quite obviously, those choices have been made without reference to CRI. The way in which colour rendering is understood by the CIE experts is clearly indicated by the definition given at the beginning of this section, but it is apparent that the preferences shown by people making visual selections of fresh produce have nothing to do with making comparisons, conscious or subconscious, with appearance under a reference source.

It can be seen that the lamp type chosen for each of the fresh produce applications imparts a particular type of colour shift, and the store operators have made themselves aware of which type of colour shift suits each type of merchandise. For the lighting designer who encounters a situation that calls for a certain type of colour shift, the available lamp data fail to provide the necessary guidance. Manufacturers give the CCT and CRI values, and also they may show the spectral power distribution curve, but nobody should assume that there is a simple relationship between this curve and colour rendering properties. Even for an experienced lighting designer, an SPD curve comprising a combination of line spectra and broad-band emissions gives little or no useful guidance on colour rendering.

What is needed is a straightforward way of showing what a lamp will do to the colour appearance of the objects that it illuminates. A lighting designer does not need to be told what is good and what is bad. The information that the designer needs is to enable an informed decision on which lamp type will best suit his or her purpose for a particular application. This leads us to the colour-mismatch vector.

The colour-mismatch vector (CMV) method

In 1988, two lamp engineers at Philips Lighting in the Netherlands proposed a novel way of presenting colour rendering information (van Kemanade and van der Burgt, 1988). Figure 4.10(a) shows the chromaticity shifts for a set of 215 colours more or less equally spaced over the chromaticity chart, when illuminated by a reference source and then by a test source. The individual colour-mismatch vectors are plotted onto the CIELAB chart, and in this case, the test lamp is a halophosphate fluorescent lamp not very different from the one represented in Figure 4.9. Each vector indicates the extent and direction of the mismatch between the reference source and the test lamp. A vector pointing towards the centre of the chart indicates a chroma reduction, and a radial direction indicates a hue shift. It should be noted that the vectors are not randomly scattered but show a distinct flow pattern, and it should not come as a surprise that mismatches increase for higher chroma, that is to say, for TCS points further from the centre.

The main features of the flow pattern are expressed in Figure 4.10(b) and (c). The hue angle on these graphs is measured from $a\star$ anticlockwise, so relationship to the unique hues can be read from Figure 4.10(a). It is clear to see whereabouts on the hue circle a test lamp introduces hue shifts or changes in chroma. The authors included more charts for fluorescent lamps with different colour rendering properties, and an interesting comparison of white SON and metal halide.

At first this type of chart may appear intimidating, but with a little practice, the wealth of information that it provides is easily extracted. There is still the comparison with a reference source, but instead of the system deciding what is good or bad, it is for the lighting designer to choose the colour rendering characteristics that will suit a particular application. Quite apart from those fresh produce supermarket displays, how else does a designer select the most suitable lamp for an indoor swimming pool, or a make-up mirror, or an orchid display, or an exhibition of antique manuscripts, or an ice-cold vodka bar? The CMV method enables designers to make informed lamp selections based on colour rendering characteristics. Unfortunately, lamp manufacturers are showing themselves to be reluctant to provide this information, particularly for the newer generation of light sources.

Colour gamut area

It might seem that an ideal light source would produce a CMV diagram in which every vector radiates outwards from the central point, creating a colourful world in which all colours appear more saturated, and there is evidence to indicate that people do prefer light sources that tend to increase colour saturation, at least to some extent.

A colour gamut is the polygon formed when the eight TCSs, illuminated by a given light source, are plotted onto the CIE UCS diagram. Equal distances between points on this diagram correspond approximately to equal perceived colour differences, so that the relative areas of the polygons formed by connecting the TCS points for a given source provide an indication of the 'colourfulness' associated with that source. Figure 4.11 shows the colour gamuts for a range of widely used light sources, and the general trend of

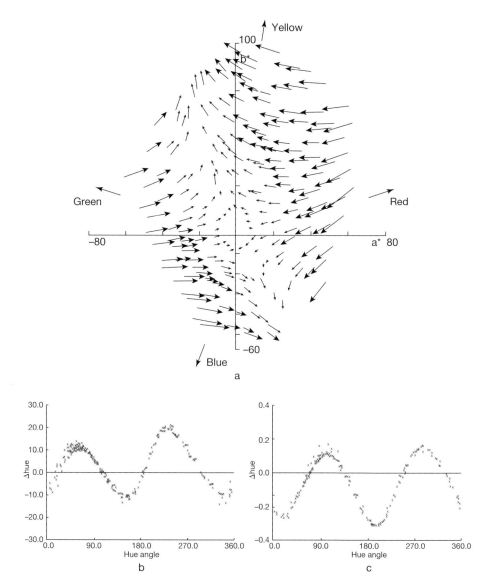

FIGURE 4.10   Colour-mismatch vector data for a halophosphate Cool White colour 33 fluorescent lamp (From van Kemenade and van der Burgt, 1988).

A)   CMVs on the CIELAB chart for Opstelten's set of 215 test colour samples.

B)   Hue component of CMV, where +ive ΔHue indicates shift to higher hue angles.

C)   Relative chroma content of CMV, where $\Delta C^\star = \Delta$chroma/chroma, and +ive $\Delta C^\star$ indicates increase in saturation with respect to reference source.

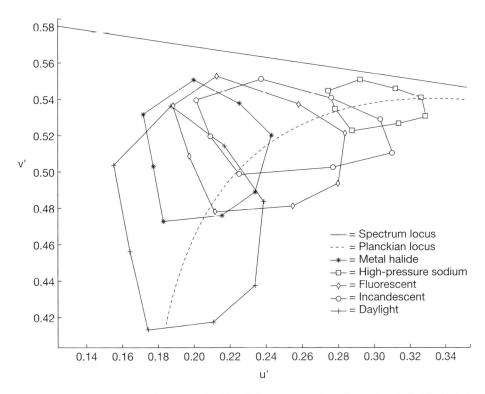

FIGURE 4.11 Gamut areas for some familiar light sources plotted on the CIE 1976 UCS (uniform chromaticity scale) diagram. Gamut area relates to the perceived 'colourfulness' associated with a light source (from Boyce, 2014).

increasing gamut areas with increasing CCT is clearly evident. Note the large area of the Daylight source, actually the CIE D65 daylight standard, and it becomes evident why this source is often regarded as the light source against which all others should be judged.

Boyce (2003) has noted a correspondence between gamut areas and findings from research studies into the phenomenon of 'visual clarity' (Bellchambers and Godby, 1972). Although this concept has never been precisely defined, a variety of studies have found that when subjects compare adjacent scenes and are instructed to adjust the light level in one 'so that the overall clarity of the scene is the same' as in the other, a lower illuminance is set in the scene with greater colour gamut area. Boyce's formula for predicting the illuminance ratio for matching appearance from the gamut area ratio is:

$$E_1 / E_2 = 1.0 - 0.61 \, log_{10}(G_1 / G_2) \qquad (4.6)$$

where E_1 and E_2 are the illuminance values and G_1 and G_2 are the gamut areas for the two light sources.

Quite separately, Rea (2013) has reported that CRI does not reliably predict people's colour preferences for fruit, vegetables, skin and other often-encountered natural objects, and has proposed that light source gamut areas should also be taken into account. The gamut areas calculated from the u', v' values of the UCS diagram produce very small values, leading him to propose a gamut area index:

$$GAI = 100(G_S / G_{ees})\qquad\qquad(4.7)$$

where G_S is the gamut area of light source S, and G_{ees} is the gamut area for an equal energy source, for which the value has been calculated to be 0.007354. The value of GAI may be more or less than 100 according to the gamut area of S, and Rea advises that for preferred appearance of natural objects, which, of course, includes other people, light sources should be 'high in CRI *and* high (but not too high) in GAI'. This leads to his proposal for 'Class A' colour for general illumination light sources, for which the chromaticity should lie on the 'white' source locus (Figure 4.7), *and* CRI should be equal to or more than 80, *and* GAI should be between 80 and 100 (Rea, 2013). For specification writers, a statement along the lines of 'All light sources shall be of Class A colour' could be expected to improve reliability.

Source spectrum and human response

At first sight, this review of how the spectral properties of illumination may influence people's responses to a lit scene might seem to comprise a bewildering array of disconnected factors, some of which have backgrounds of intensive research while others are based on not much more than casual observation. However, some introspection suggests an underlying pattern that gives some insight into how these factors are connected.

It is clear that when we are concerned with a brightness response rather than visibility, $V(\lambda)$ tends to underrate sources that are rich in the shorter visible wavelengths, that is to say, sources that are high in S/P ratio and CCT. While it has long been recognised that this occurs for scotopic conditions, the $B(\lambda)$ function (Formula 4.2) applies for photopic conditions as well. The $V_{B3}(\lambda)$ function (Figure 4.2) has been proposed as the appropriate illumination metric for indoor general lighting practice, but has yet to gain acceptance.

Illumination that has high luminous efficiency on the B3 metric would also provide well for circadian response, measured on the $V_C(\lambda)$ function (Figure 4.4), making it an appropriate source for daytime illumination. Light sources with CCT values around 4000K are commonly described as 'white' light sources, and it may be noted that this is the CCT value at which the 'white' source locus crosses the black-body locus (Figure 4.7), suggesting that higher CCT sources with chromaticities on the 'white' source locus might not attract the negative assessments accorded to the high S/P sources used in recent research studies. The usefulness of the high retinal image resolution associated with high S/P sources has been questioned, but it would seem reasonable to suppose that 'white' high S/P sources would gain any such advantages without incurring negative assessments for appearance.

McCandless' notion of 'sunlight and skylight' suggests options for attractive effects by adding low S/P highlights to overall high S/P illumination, and the Kruithof effect points to high S/P (or CCT) illumination gaining preference at high illuminance levels, in other words, high CCTs for daytime and low CCTs for night time. All of this fits in with providing illumination to coincide with the circadian cycle.

Rea's proposal that, for general lighting practice, the shortcomings of CRI may be largely overcome by specifying 'Class A' colour defines a basis for generally preferred colour rendering. Figure 4.11 shows clearly how, for high CRI sources, gamut area (related to colourfulness) tends to increase with CCT. While CRI relates to the 'naturalness' of colour appearance, Rea's proposal adds a new notion of 'whiteness', and, through including GAI in the criteria, the appearance of 'colourfulness'. This may, in turn, be seen to be consistent with the 'visual clarity' concept, and furthermore, with the other more anecdotal concepts observed by McCandless and Kruithof. In this way, the range of factors reviewed in this chapter may be seen as contributing towards a reasonable and consistent understanding of human response to light source spectrum.

Even so, a designer who wishes to have control over the appearance of a space, or selected targets within the space, is left in a difficult situation. He or she cannot avoid feeling poorly supported by the information currently available from the lighting industry, and it is perhaps ironic that efforts to improve this situation tend to be resisted by the industry on the grounds that such changes would cause confusion.

My own approach has been to equip myself with a *GretagMacbeth ColorChecker*, and to use this to make objective assessments of the colour characteristics of light sources. The *ColorChecker* comprises 24 matt-surfaced colour samples mounted on a stiff board, and some time needs to be spent examining it under mid-day daylight, as shown in Figure 4.12. The bottom row is a grey scale, from full-white to full-black, and in this viewing

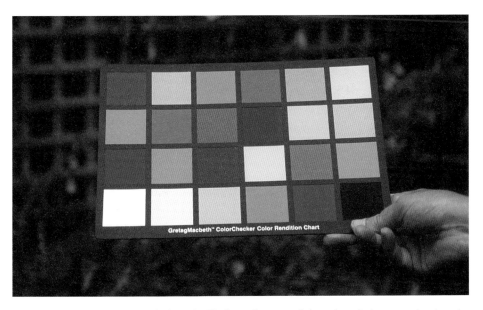

FIGURE 4.12 The *GretagMacbeth ColorChecker* colour rendition chart being examined under daylight. A viewer who forms a clear memory image of the chart in this situation can then make comparisons with its appearance under other sources of illumination.

condition all the samples appear neutral (no hint of hue), and the steps between them appear equally spaced. The next row up comprises primary colours, with the additive primaries to the left and the subtractive primaries to the right, and all of them appear as fully saturated, clear colours. The two rows above are moderate colours, some with special significance. For example, starting from the left-hand end of the top row, the samples represent dark skin, light skin, blue sky, foliage and so on. Explanations are given on the reverse side.

Start by gaining experience of the appearance of the *ColorChecker* under daylight. This gives you a tool that enables you to objectively assess the colour characteristics of other light sources and illumination conditions, whether you are evaluating a sample of new type of light source or visiting a recent lighting installation. The appearance of the *ColorChecker* will quickly reveal to you how your perception of colours is influenced by the illumination. It is worth noting that under low light levels, all the colours will appear dull and the intervals between the grey samples will appear compressed towards the darker end. Providing that illumination is sufficient to ensure photopic adaptation, the appearance of the primaries can be particularly revealing. While you will be accustomed to all of these samples appearing saturated, certain light sources can cause some of them to appear unexpectedly bright. To understand this, think back to the discussion of lamps used to enhance the appearance of various types of food displays. More generally, look carefully at the appearances of the moderate colours, noting that people are particularly sensitive about skin colours. When people complain about colour rendering, the most commonly occurring comments are of the 'They make you look awful!' type.

It is in this way that a lighting designer may select lamp types for various applications with confidence that the effect on the appearances of coloured room surfaces and objects will be in accord with the overall design objectives. From the foregoing discussion, it is clear that people have different expectations for daytime and night time illumination, and where the aim is to satisfy those expectations, the designer should provide for coincidence with the circadian cycle. Of course, circumstances will occur where the intention is to achieve alertness and visual stimulation when people would naturally be inclined to restfulness, and for these applications the intensity and duration of bright light exposure needs to be given consideration. Meanwhile it is to be expected that developments in light source technology will provide designers with increased options, and it is to be hoped that the lighting industry will respond with more useful product information. In particular, that it will recognise that while the needs of specifiers may be best met by familiar, single figure values, designers' needs are more complex. They need information that addresses the foregoing issues, and this is not met by catalogue pages presenting brightly coloured spectral power distribution curves.

References

Bellchambers, H.E. and A.C. Godby (1972). Illumination, colour rendering and visual clarity. *Lighting Research and Technology*, 4: 104–106.

Berman, S.M., G. Fein, D.I. Jewett and F. Ashford (1993). Luminance-controlled pupil size affects Landolt C task performance. *Journal of the Illuminating Engineering Society*, 22: 150–165.

Boyce, P.R. (2014). *Human Factors in Lighting, Third edition*. Boca Raton, FL: CRC Press.

Commission Internationale de l'Eclairage (CIE) (1987). *International Lighting Vocabulary*, item 845-02-59, CIE 17.4-1987.

——(1994). *Method of Measuring and Specifying Colour Rendering*, CIE 13.3-1994.

Davis, W. and Y. Ohno (2004). Towards an improved color rendering metric. *Proceedings of the 5th International Conference on Solid State Lighting*, SPIE 5941.

Fairchild, M.D. (2004). *Color Appearance Models, Second edition*. Chichester: John Wiley & Sons.

Illuminating Engineering Society of North America (IESNA) (2000). *The IESNA Lighting Handbook, Ninth Edition*.

Kruithof, A.A. (1941). Tubular luminescence lamps for general illumination. *Philips Technical Review*, 6(2): 65–73.

McCandless, S.R. (1958). *A Method of Lighting for the Stage (4th edn)*. New York: Theatre Art Books.

Rea, M.S. (2013). *Value Metrics for Better Lighting*. Bellingham, WA: SPIE Press.

Rea, M.S. and J.P. Freyssinier (2013). White lighting for residential applications. *Lighting Research and Technology*, 45(3): 331–344.

Rea, M.S., L.C. Radetsky and J.D. Bullough (2011). Towards a model of outdoor scene brightness. *Lighting Research and Technology*, 43(1): 7–30.

Van Kemanade, J.T.C. and P.J.M. van der Burgt (1988). Light sources and colour rendering: Additional information to the R_a index. *Proceedings of the CIBSE National Lighting Conference*, Cambridge, UK, pp.133–143.

Wei, M., K.W. Houser, B. Orland, D.H. Lang, N. Ram, M.J. Sliwinski and M. Bose (2014). *Field study of office worker responses to fluorescent lighting of different CCT and lumen output*. J. Environ. Psychol., http://dx.doi.org/10.1016//j.envp,2014.04.009

5

SPATIAL ILLUMINATION DISTRIBUTIONS

Chapter summary

The appearances of three-dimensional objects are influenced by the lighting patterns that are generated through interactions between the objects and the spatial distribution of illumination. As noted in Chapter 1, there are three types of these object lighting patterns; shading, highlight and shadow patterns; and they appear superimposed over each object's surface in response to the optical characteristics of the objects and the photometric characteristics of the surrounding light field. The light field is also examined in terms of perceived characteristics, and the concepts of the *'flow' and the 'sharpness' of illumination* are discussed. These characteristics may have the effects of revealing, or enhancing or subduing the appearance of selected object attributes. The perceived strength of the 'flow' of light relates to the vector/scalar ratio (VSR) and its perceived direction corresponds with the vector direction. The highlight contrast potential (HCP) gives an indication of the extent to which lighting may provide for perceived 'sharpness'.

Three-dimensional distributions of illumination

In Chapter 1, we noted that the green cylinder interacted with the illumination distribution to produce lighting patterns that appeared superimposed onto the surface of the cylinder and the checker board (Figure 1.1), and these patterns not only affected the cylinder's appearance, but they influenced our whole understanding of the surrounding light field and the objects within it. In this chapter we are going to look closely at these lighting patterns, and we are going to identify the three-dimensional characteristics of illumination that cause them.

The three object lighting patterns

The three objects shown in Figure 5.1 are all interacting with the same surrounding light field, but the object lighting patterns produced by those interactions are strikingly different. The matt white sphere has formed a graded *shading pattern* of varying surface illuminance related to surface orientation, and in this respect, the pattern follows from the cosine law of illumination. Completely different in appearance is the *highlight pattern* generated by the glossy black sphere, which is formed by specular images of the higher luminance elements in this space that are also the sources of illumination. Different again is the *shadow pattern* produced by the peg-on-a-disc, where the shadow cast by the peg is clearly revealed on the disc's surface (Cuttle, 1971).

Each of these lighting patterns tells us something different about the three-dimensional light field surrounding these objects. Look carefully at the matt white sphere. No part of its surface is unlit, but there is a distinct bias. If I could hand you a small arrow, you would be able to place it on the image to coincide with your perception of the direction of the 'flow' of light. It would not matter how many sources of illumination are present, always you would perceive just one 'flow' direction. You might also describe the apparent strength of the 'flow' as being distinct, but not strong. Now turn to the glossy black

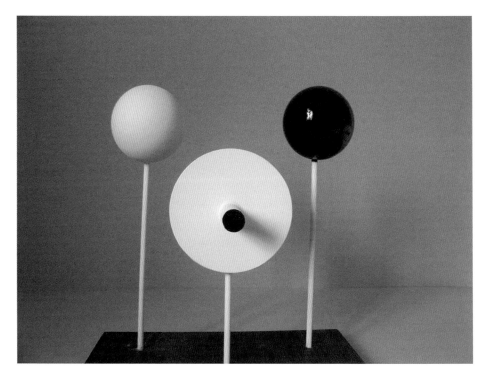

FIGURE 5.1   The triple object lighting patterns device. This device separates as far as possible the three object lighting patterns. The matt white sphere shows the shading pattern; the glossy black sphere shows the highlight pattern; and the peg-on-a-disc shows the shadow pattern.

sphere. Its appearance is dominated by a single 'highlight' image, and if you look carefully you will be able to make out the shape of this light source's outline and recognise that it is a window. No other light source is bright enough to register a noticeable 'highlight', and so you may conclude that the window is the sole source of direct illumination. Finally, look at the shadow pattern formed on the peg-on-a-disc. Its direction coincides with the appearance of the 'flow' direction, and like the shading pattern, it is only moderately strong. Also, it is quite softy defined, as this lighting lacks 'sharpness'.

You will have worked out by now that you have been looking at lighting patterns generated by the light field in a small, or moderately sized, room with fairly light (reflective) room surfaces, lit by a single side-window. This is a pretty detailed description of the location and the light field within it. What would be the effect if we leave the triple-object in its present position but change the lighting?

Figure 5.1 reappears as Figure 5.2(a), and below it, you see the effect of blanking off the window and introducing a spotlight in Figure 5.2(b), and then turning off the spotlight and adding six small display lights in Figure 5.2(c). The two columns of photos across to the right show the effects of these lighting conditions on the appearance of two groups of objects. The first column shows a group of familiar domestic items, and we should appreciate that, even for objects that we are unlikely to select for display treatment, their appearance can be substantially affected by lighting. In fact, the appearance of everything that we see, pick up and make use of is affected by the object lighting patterns formed by its surrounding light field. Figure 5.2(d) shows the garlic pot and two capsicums in the daylight situation, which has a distinct 'flow' of light without 'sharpness'. The effect of the single spotlight in Figure 5.2(e) is to reproduce quite closely the 'flow' direction while somewhat increasing the 'flow' strength, but the really noticeable change is the presence of 'sharpness', revealed by the highlight (even more noticeable in real life than it appears in this image) and shading patterns. In Figure 5.2(f), the 'flow' revealed by the shading pattern on the garlic pot has almost vanished, but the effect of 'sharpness' due to the lighting is still highly evident.

The second column of photos shows some objects that we might put on display to attract interest, and here the object attributes include transparency, iridescence, and dichromatic colours. These three figures, 5.2(g), (h) and (i), call for careful attention. How would you approach the task of providing display lighting for this group of objects? At first it might seem that almost anything could work, but it should be noted that the three object lighting patterns, being the shading, highlight and shadow patterns, are separately identifiable and it is the different balances of these patterns that determine the spatial lighting effects. Careful observation of these images shows how the attributes of any one of these objects may be revealed, enhanced or subdued by the balance of object lighting patterns created by their interactions with the light field.

To summarise, we have identified **_three object lighting patterns:_**

    The Shading Pattern: Due to the interaction of an object's three-dimensional form with a 'flow' of light. The pattern is a variation of surface illuminance due to changing incidence of light with surface orientation which influences the appearance of object form and texture. The lighting metrics that relate to the 'flow' are the vector/scalar

Triple patterns device

The 'daylight' condition

(a)

Single spotlight condition

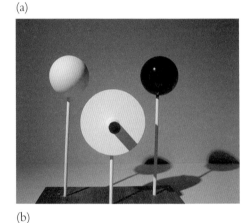

(b)

Multiple display lights condition

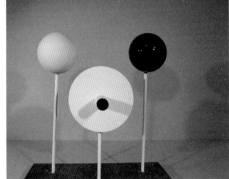

(c)

FIGURE 5.2 For the three lighting conditions described in the text; the first column of photos shows the lighting patterns formed on the triple lighting patterns device, and the next two columns show the lighting patterns on a group of domestic objects and a group of display objects.

(d)

(g)

(e)

(h)

(f)

(i)

ratio (VSR), which corresponds with the perceived strength of 'flow', and the vector direction, which corresponds with the perceived direction of 'flow'.

The Highlight Pattern: Due to specular reflections of relatively high luminance objects, particularly light sources, that appear superimposed on an object's surface. There has to be some level of surface gloss for a highlight pattern to be evident, and either polished metals or shiny, dark coloured surfaces give maximum effect. This pattern influences the appearance of gloss, sheen or lustre, and may be described as an aspect of the 'sharpness' of lighting. The metric that relates to these effects is the highlight contrast potential (HCP).

The Shadow Pattern: Due to a shadow caster projecting a shadow onto a receiving surface in a directional light field. The appearance of this lighting pattern may be described in terms of both the strength and 'sharpness' of cast shadows, and it may influence the perception of object form, texture and/or location. Perceived shadow strength is associated with the VSR, and 'sharpness' with the HCP.

The concept of object lighting patterns is readily understood by non-lighting people and can form a useful basis for discussion when lighting designers are talking about how their proposals will affect the appearance of the various objects that will form significant components of the design. Designers are usually able to communicate their ideas using these concepts without going into details, such as explaining the precise difference between a shading pattern and a shadow pattern. However, while non-lighting people will perceive the lighting patterns entirely as a visual effect, for designers, there is a deeper insight. Every lighting pattern is recognised to be a three-dimensional interaction between a particular type of surface and a particular type of incident light. The understanding that there are just three types of object lighting patterns – shading, highlight and shadow – and two lighting characteristics of concern – 'flow' and 'sharpness' – provides powerful concepts for devising distributions of light that respond to space, form and material.

To appreciate how these concepts might be applied in the real world, we will take a look at the lighting for an up-market retail store. QELA offers high couture fashion in the setting of an exclusive art gallery, and is located in Doha, on the Pearl, which is a man-made archipelago off the coast of Qatar. The entrance from a shopping mall gives no view to the interior, giving a sense of entering into a private zone. The initial view of the central atrium, shown in Figure 5.3, with its freestanding staircase connecting the two floors, has been designed to create a strong visual impact. Here, selected displays of beautiful accessories are presented within the setting of an art gallery, and all of this contained by the curved forms of the architecture and the overarching domed ceiling.

The design brief had stated that "merchandise was to stand out from the ambient effect with highly controlled accent lighting". The lighting designers, Gary Campbell and Tommaso Gimigliano of dpa lighting design, proceeded to devise separate lighting solutions specifically for each aspect of the overall design. In the interests of controllability and energy efficiency, it was decided that lighting throughout the store was to be LED-based and dimmable, although some exceptions were made for the jewellery displays and decorative fittings.

FIGURE 5.3   The striking first view of the interior of the QELA boutique, Doha, where high quality accessories are presented in the setting of an art gallery, calling for a variety of lighting characteristics. Interior design by UXUS Design, Amsterdam; Photography by Adrian Haddad; Lighting by dpa lighting design.

The immediate impression is one of a bright and lively space. A MRSE level of at least $300 \, \text{lm/m}^2$ is required to give this sense of a distinctly bright space, and it can be seen that while there are areas of white or near-white surfaces, overall reflectance values are varied and include some quite dark surfaces. Note particularly the floor, which although highly polished, is nonetheless highly absorptive, which will have the effect of increasing the perceived strength of the downward 'flow' of light. However, the high MRSE value requires a high level of first reflected flux (FRF), and to achieve this without wasting light calls for luminaire flux to be directed onto high reflectance (low absorptance) surfaces.

Taking a closer look at the central area, Figure 5.4 shows how direct flux is strongly concentrated onto the displays. This central zone is lit from the ceiling above the atrium, and this involves throws of nine or ten metres. The 'flow' of light is strongly downwards and its 'sharpness' creates glittering highlight patterns on the polished metals and richly glossy surfaces of the luxury goods on display, as well as crisp, sharply defined shadow patterns. These lighting patterns are set into contrast by the display podiums, which lack any surface features that respond to 'sharpness'. Their smooth, matt surfaces reveal shading patterns, but not highlight patterns.

A quite different lighting distribution is provided for the background to these displays, which is formed by the perimeter walls and the artworks supported on them. These are washed by angled overhead lighting, which delivers much of the FRF for the space. As for the domed ceiling, these are surfaces for which distinct lighting patterns are not wanted.

Moving into the smaller surrounding areas, even more strongly accentuated display lighting effects are achieved on the mannequins as a result of the much reduced ambient

FIGURE 5.4 QELA – The display lighting in the central area has strong downward 'flow', with 'sharpness' creating crisp shadow and highlight patterns, set against a background of artwork displays. Interior design by UXUS Design, Amsterdam; Photography by Adrian Haddad; Lighting by dpa lighting design.

illumination, as shown in Figures 5.5 and 5.6. 'Flow' directions are still vertically downwards, and this lighting creates particularly strong shading and highlight patterns.

Some subtle changes are revealed upon ascending the staircase to the upper level. Warm white illumination is used throughout the store, and, as shown in Figure 5.7, this sense of warmth is reinforced by the flames of simulated open fire. To the left of this view, the jewellery displays receive special treatment. The freestanding podiums include integrated fibre optic downlights in the slim polished chrome ring at the top, and these are powered by metal halide projectors adjustable for both intensity and colour. 'Sharpness' is essential for the strong highlight patterns that give jewellery its sparkle, and cool white illumination is best for viewing silver and diamond pieces.

LED sources, ceiling recessed and track mounted, are used extensively, and all may be dimmed by remote devices. In addition, staff can adjust display luminaires for direction, both pan and tilt, as well as for intensity, from an iPad, giving them free rein to achieve creative lighting effects.

Clearly the ability to envisage lighting in three dimensions is crucial to understanding how to evolve design proposals to create light fields to interact with the surfaces and objects that make up our surroundings. The three lighting patterns provide a useful basis not only for describing visual effects that a proposed lighting distribution will achieve, but also for thinking through the characteristic of lighting that will do the job. For those proposals to be effective, they need to have photometric validity.

FIGURE 5.5 QELA – In this display area, which is adjacent to the central area, the lower mean room surface exitance (MRSE) level has the effect of strengthening the shading patterns. Interior design by UXUS Design, Amsterdam; Photography by Adrian Haddad; Lighting by dpa lighting design.

FIGURE 5.6 QELA – In this display area, the mannequin appears isolated by the strong shading pattern generated by the selective lighting. Interior design by UXUS Design, Amsterdam; Photography by Adrian Haddad; Lighting by dpa lighting design.

FIGURE 5.7   QELA – On the upper floor, the 'fire' on the right matches the warm white illumination used throughout the boutique, except for the jewellery display area on the left, where the colour temperature as well as the intensity of the display lighting can be adjusted to suit the items on display. Interior design by UXUS Design, Amsterdam; Photography by Adrian Haddad; Lighting by dpa lighting design.

Three-dimensional illumination distributions

There are distinct differences between measuring illumination at a point on a surface and at a point in space. The CIE (International Commission on Illumination) defines illuminance in terms of incidence at a point on a surface, and the familiar cosine-corrected illumination meter is designed specifically for measuring that quantity. The CIE definition simplifies illumination into a two-dimensional concept, but this has not been achieved without consequence.

It is conventional for illumination to be measured, calculated and specified in terms of illuminance on two-dimensional planes, such as visual task planes and wall-to-wall horizontal working planes, and this is severely limiting for design options (Lam, 1977). Conversely, the 'flow' of light is a three-dimensional concept, and it involves quite different thinking about lighting. Instead of planes, think of the volume of a space comprising a light field that fully occupies the space, and three-dimensional objects within the space interacting with the light field to generate object lighting patterns that appear superimposed on their surfaces. The appearance of 'flow' is made evident by shading patterns and by the strength of shadow patterns, and may be perceived to vary in both strength and direction throughout the space. Leaving aside 'sharpness' for the moment, we need to be able to measure the spatial distribution of illumination at any chosen point within the space in order to examine this effect.

Consider the point P as a point in space with its location defined by the three mutually perpendicular axes, x, y, and z, as shown in Figure 5.8. Figure 5.9 shows a section through P in the plane of the z axis and the point source S1, which is the sole source of illumination at P. A solid plane passing through P is rotated for maximum illuminance on surface A, and for this condition, the distance shown at P to the perimeter of the illumination solid is proportional to $E_{A(max)}$. Rotation of the plane from this direction causes E_A to reduce in proportion to the cosine of the rotation angle, so that when the angle exceeds 90°, $E_A = 0$.

In this way, the circular form in Figure 5.9 can be envisaged as an illumination solid that forms a three-dimensional representation of the distribution of E_A, and for this special case of the illumination distribution due to a single point source, the illumination solid is a three-dimensional cosine distribution, represented by a sphere whose surface passes through the reference point, and for which a diameter from the reference point coincides with the direction of the source. It can be seen that the illumination distribution about P is totally asymmetric, so that if a small three-dimensional object is placed at P, one side will be illuminated and the other side will be in total darkness. This illumination difference on opposite sides of an object is of interest. If, instead of recording the distribution of E_A, we record the distribution of $(E_A - E_B)$, that is to say, the difference on opposite sides of the plane, the solid would be unchanged because when surface A is facing away from S1, $(E_A - E_B)$ would have a negative value.

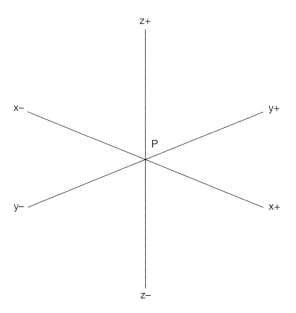

FIGURE 5.8 The point P is located at the intersection of the x, y and z orthogonal axes. The x and y axes are in the horizontal plane, and the z axis is vertical. Unless otherwise specified, it is convenient to assume a direction of view from the y-direction ('eye' direction), so that x is 'a-cross'. While any other view direction may be possible, this simple convention tends to avoid errors.

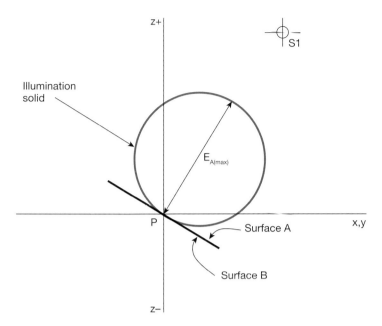

FIGURE 5.9   The three-dimensional illumination distribution about point P due to the small source S1 is defined by a spherical illumination solid, where the length of $E_{A(max)}$ is proportional to the illuminance on surface A when normal to the direction of S1.

Figure 5.10 shows the effect of adding a second point source S2. In this case, the blue contours show parts of the illumination solids for the individual sources, but where the solids coincide, the value of $(E_A - E_B)$ is shown by the red contour. The values of $E_{A\,max}$ and for S1 and S2 are shown as vectors, and the value of the resultant vector, $(E_A - E_B)_{max}$, is given by completing the vector parallelogram. It can be seen that the red contour is similar to the illumination solid for the single point source, meaning that the distribution of illuminance difference on opposite sides of the plane is identical to that produced by a point source. If this happens when we add a second source, it will happen when we add a third, or fourth ... or an infinite number of sources. We have established the point that at any illuminated point in space, the distribution of illuminance difference in opposite directions $(E_A - E_B)$ may be represented as an illumination vector. This concept is attributed to Professor A.A. Gershun, whose book, *The Light Field*, was published (in Russian) in 1936.

In Figure 5.11, we move from hypothetical situations to a real situation. The blue contour is typical of an illumination solid that might occur in an indoor location illuminated predominantly from overhead, but with a sideways bias as might occur near a dark coloured wall. The contour is smooth because it is the sum of spherical solids due to every luminous element surrounding the measurement point. Illumination solid contours cannot display sharp peaks or troughs. The red contour is the distribution of $(E_A - E_B)$, and the plane passing through P has been rotated as previously, but this time the aim has been to find the direction that gives maximum illuminance difference on opposite sides of the

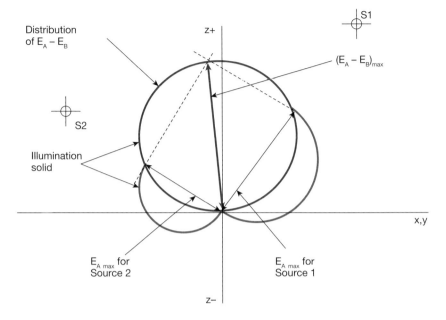

FIGURE 5.10 The illumination solid is now the sum of component solids due to sources S1 and S2, but the distribution of $E_A - E_B$ is a spherical solid, identical in form, but not magnitude or direction, to the illumination solid due to S1 alone.

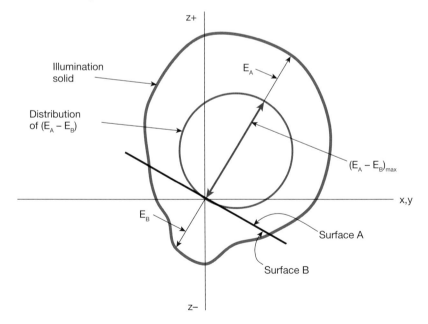

FIGURE 5.11 The illumination solid at a point in a space where light arrives from every direction, but predominately from overhead although with a sideways bias. Despite the irregularity of the illumination solid, the distribution $E_A - E_B$ is defined by a spherical solid identical in form to the illumination solid produced previously by S1.

plane, which may not coincide with the maximum value of the illumination solid contour. Rotation of the plane from this direction would cause $(E_A - E_B)$ to reduce in proportion to the cosine of the rotation angle, so that when the rotation angle equals $90°$, $E_A = E_B$. The distribution of $(E_A - E_B)$ is a three-dimensional cosine distribution identical in form to the illumination solid due to a single point source. As shown in Figure 5.8, the x, y axis lies in the horizontal plane, and the z axis is vertical.

We are now in a position to analyse the illumination distribution about a point in space into its two components. In Figure 5.12 the maximum value of $(E_A - E_B)$ and the direction in which this value occurs define the illumination vector **E.** For any plane passing through P, the illuminance difference on opposite surfaces equals the vector component on the axis normal to the plane. For the horizontal plane through P, $\mathbf{E}_{(z)} = E_{(z+)} - E_{(z-)}$, and similarly, for a vertical plane through P normal to the x axis, the magnitude of the illumination vector component is $\mathbf{E}_{(x)}$. Note that the symbol for a vector is shown in bold type, and while this distinction is clearly indicated in print, in manuscript it is made by a small arrow over the E. Note that a vector is defined in terms of both magnitude and direction. The distribution of the vector component is defined by the three-dimensional vector solid, which, as we have noted, is always a spherical cosine distribution with its surface passing through P and its diameter equal to the vector magnitude.

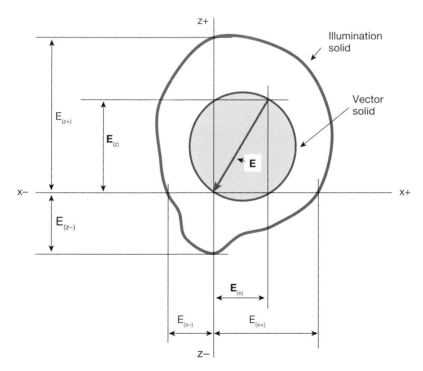

FIGURE 5.12   The magnitude and direction of $(E_A - E_B)_{max}$ defines the illumination vector, which is depicted as an arrow acting towards the point. The vector in turn is defined by its components on the x, y, and z axes. The vector solid accounts entirely for the asymmetry of the illumination solid.

In Figure 5.13, the vector solid has been subtracted from the illumination solid and what remains is a three-dimensional solid that is divided by the axis normal to the vector direction. This solid has point symmetry about P, that is to say, for any axis through P, the distance to the contour of this solid in one direction equals the distance in the opposite direction. This is the symmetric solid, and while it may depart from uniformity, the illuminance due to the symmetric solid ~E in any direction from P is equal to ~E in the opposite direction. If a plane passing through P is rotated, for every orientation, the illuminance values on opposite sides of the plane due to the symmetric solid will be equal. In other words, it is the solid for which $E_A - E_B = 0$ for every orientation.

In this way, we arrive at the following conclusions:

1   That at any illuminated point in space, the three-dimensional distribution of illuminance may be defined by an illumination solid.
2   The illumination solid is the sum of two component solids: the vector solid and the symmetric solid.
3   The vector solid is a spherical cosine distribution, and is defined by the magnitude and direction of the illumination vector **E**. The illuminance distribution at the reference point P represented by the vector solid is identical to the distribution that would be produced by a single compact source located in the vector direction.
4   The symmetric solid has the property that, for any plane passing through P, it produces equal illuminance ~E on opposite sides.

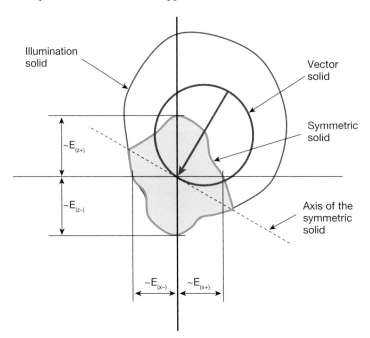

FIGURE 5.13   If the vector solid is subtracted from the illumination solid, what is left is a solid that is symmetrical in every direction about the point. This is the symmetric solid.

5   The visible characteristics of the illuminance distribution over the unobstructed surface of a three-dimensional object that is small in relation to the surrounding light field may be analysed as the sum of distributions due to the vector and symmetric components, one being entirely asymmetrical about the measurement point, and the other entirely symmetrical.

6   Two special cases may be noted:

- For a single point source, the illumination solid is coincident with the vector solid, and the symmetric component ~E = 0.
- For an integrating sphere, the illumination solid is coincident with the symmetric solid, comprising ideally a spherical distribution centred at P, and the illumination vector **E** = 0.

To all of the above, I wish to add a personal observation. The concept that the spatial distribution of illumination at any illuminated point in space comprises two components – one of which is entirely asymmetric about the point and could be produced by a compact source in the direction of the vector, while the other is entirely symmetric about the point – is not intuitive. It emerges from a mathematical analysis, and is, in my opinion, the most remarkable finding to emerge from the study of illumination engineering. It provides a unique design insight, and if you look for it, you can see it.

Illumination solids and the 'flow' of light

Look back to Figure 5.2, and note particularly the changing appearance of the matt white sphere in the three lighting conditions. This object forms a different shading pattern with each variation of the light field and, every time, the appearance of the shading pattern can be described in terms of the apparent strength and direction of the 'flow' of light. Equally, it may be described in terms of different relationships of the asymmetric and symmetric components of the illumination solid. We have here the basis of a means for assessing lighting according to its potential to influence the appearance of three-dimensional objects through the creation of shading patterns, which in turn, may be described in terms of the 'flow' of light.

If an object is small enough in relation to its surrounding environment for us to be able to examine its illumination by considering the illumination distribution at a point, then we can think of every element visible from the point to be contributing its own mini-vector at the point. We have two alternative ways of summing these mini-vectors. If we sum them individually, we have the illumination solid. If we sum their opposite differences, the sum of these individual vectors is always a single vector that defines the magnitude and direction of the (asymmetric) vector solid. The difference between the illumination solid and the vector solid is the symmetric solid. It should be apparent that if the vector solid is large in relation to the symmetric solid, then the 'flow' of light will appear to be strong. It might seem, therefore, that the ratio of asymmetric to symmetric solids would provide a useful index of this effect, but it would have a range from zero to infinity, which is inconvenient. In mathematics, a vector quantity is one that has both magnitude and direction, while a quantity that has magnitude only is termed a scalar. It was with this in mind that J.A. Lynes proposed the concept of scalar illuminance, which is defined in terms of the average illuminance over the whole surface of a small sphere centred at a reference point (Lynes *et al.*, 1966). It follows that for any illumination solid, the scalar illuminance will be the sum of contributions from the vector and symmetric solids. The contribution from the symmetric solid will be equal to the symmetric illuminance ~E, and from Figure 5.14 is can be seen that the asymmetric solid will contribute one-quarter of the vector magnitude, so that scalar illuminance:

$$E_{sr} = \frac{\mathbf{E}}{4} + \sim E$$

(5.1)

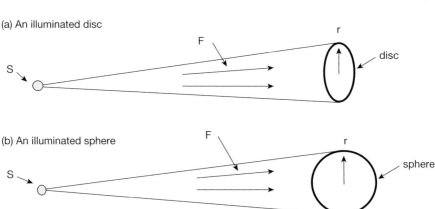

(a) An illuminated disc

(b) An illuminated sphere

FIGURE 5.14 In (a), a small source S projects luminous flux of F lm onto a disc of radius r, producing a surface illuminance E = F/(π.r²). In (b), the disc is replaced by a sphere of radius r, giving a surface illuminance E = F/(4π.r²).

This enables us to specify the apparent strength of the 'flow' of light in terms of the vector/scalar ratio:

$$VSR = \mathbf{E} / E_{sr}$$

(5.2)

VSR has a scale from zero (the integrating sphere condition) to four (the point source in a black environment). Research studies in a face-to-face situation indicated preference for VSR within the range 1.2 to 1.8 (Cuttle *et al.*, 1967) and this finding has more recently been corroborated by Protzman and Houser (2005). Table 5.1 gives an approximate indication of how assessments of the perceived strength of 'flow' are likely to vary with the VSR.

Regardless of the number of light sources present, the asymmetric component resolves into a cosine distribution defined by the illumination vector, and providing that the VSR is sufficient for the 'flow' direction to be apparent, its direction coincides with the vector direction. There are two alternative ways of defining the vector direction. One is to specify vector altitude (α) and azimuth (φ) angles, where Figure 5.15(a) shows:

$$\alpha = sin^{-1}(\mathbf{E}_{(z)} / \mathbf{E})$$

(5.3)

TABLE 5.1 Vector/scalar ratio and the perceived 'flow' of light

Vector/scalar ratio	Assessment of appearance	Application
4.0 (max)		
3.5	Dramatic	
3.0	Very strong	Strong contrasts, detail in shadows not discernible
2.5	Strong	Suitable for display; too harsh for human features
2.0	Moderately strong	Pleasant appearance for distant faces (formal)
1.5	Moderately weak	Pleasant appearance for near faces (informal)
1.0	Weak	Soft lighting for subdued effects
0.5	Very weak	Flat shadow-free lighting
0 (min)		

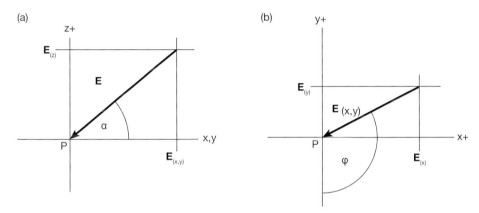

FIGURE 5.15 (a): Vertical section through P showing illumination vector altitude angle α, and (b): Horizontal section through P showing azimuth angle φ of the horizontal vector component.

There is more than one way of specifying the azimuth angle, and Figure 5.15(b) shows φ measured anticlockwise from the y- axis, as this is often taken to represent the direction of view. Care needs to be taken to cope with the full 360 degrees of rotation.

Another way is to specify the vector direction in terms of a unit vector, which assumes the vector to have unity value and expresses the direction in the form $(\mathbf{e}_{(x)}, \mathbf{e}_{(y)}, \mathbf{e}_{(z)})$, where the unit vector component on the x axis:

$$e_{(x)} = E_{(x)} / E \tag{5.4}$$

and similarly for $\mathbf{e}_{(y)}$ and $\mathbf{e}_{(z)}$. It can be seen that each of these unit vector values does in fact specify the cosine of the angle that the vector forms with the axis. While care needs to be taken over the signs of the unit vector components, this concise form of notation is recommended as largely avoiding the confusions that are likely to occur when dealing with angles greater than 2π.

The previously cited research into preferences for face-to-face viewing (Cuttle *et al.*, 1967) found distinct preference for vector altitudes in the range 15 to 45 degrees, or $0.25 < \mathbf{e}_{(z)} < 0.7$. Even more distinct was the identification of a downward 'flow' of light as the least preferred condition, for which $\alpha = 90$ degrees and $\mathbf{e} = (0,0,1)$. For face-to-face viewing situations where overhead lighting is unavoidable, VSR should be kept to a low value.

In this way, the characteristics of a three-dimensional distribution of illumination, as it may affect the perceived strength and direction of the 'flow' of light, can be specified in terms of simple photometric quantities. Procedures for predicting and measuring these quantities are described in the following chapter.

The 'sharpness' of illumination

While 'flow' relates to the appearance of the shading patterns and the density of the shadow patterns, 'sharpness' relates to the appearance of the highlight patterns and the crispness of the shadow patterns. Look back to Figure 5.2, and appreciate how differently these two lighting concepts appear.

A thought experiment

Once again, you must clear your mind of what you expect to experience and let your imagination take control. In Figure 5.16, a surface is illuminated by a diffusing disc light source. The illuminance at P is given by the disc source formula (Simons and Bean, 2001):

$$E_P = \frac{\pi L_S}{2}(1 - cos\alpha)$$

(5.5)

The subtence angle of the source, α, may have any value from a degree or two, for which the source would be close to the hypothetical point source, up to 180 degrees, at which point the source becomes a uniform diffusing hemisphere. At the point P, we place the comparison panel shown in Figure 5.17, which compares two materials, a sample of black glass and a matt white surface. This panel was originally proposed by J.A. Worthy (1990) to explain his own research into this aspect of lighting.

Imagine that as we vary α, the source luminance adjusts to maintain the illuminance E_P at a constant value of 100 lux. The appearance of the matt white surface will not change while we make this variation because its luminance remains constant, but the appearance of the black glass sample will undergo radical changes. If we start from the luminous hemisphere condition ($\alpha = 180$ degrees), the glass appears to have a grey cast over it. As α is reduced, this cast shrinks to become an image of the disc source, and around the image we see the blackness of the glass. As the image continues to shrink, it increases in brightness until it becomes an intensely bright, small dot that appears sharply defined against the blackness of the glass. The lighting now has 'sharpness', and this is revealed by the appearance of the glass, not the white disc. This effect is similar to the highlight patterns on the white and black spheres shown in Figure 5.2(a) to (c).

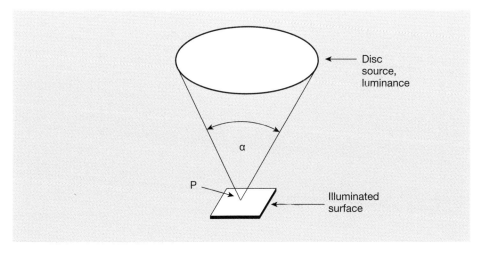

FIGURE 5.16 The point P is on a surface, and is illuminated by a disc-shaped source that is normal to the surface and of angular subtence α.

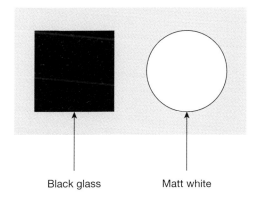

Black glass   Matt white

FIGURE 5.17 This comparison surface has two mounted samples that respond differently to the disc source. After Worthy (1990).

If we rearrange the disc source formula to $L_S = \dfrac{2E_P}{\pi(1 - cos\alpha)}$, Figure 5.18 shows how the value of L_S has to be varied to maintain $E_P = 100$ lx. It can be seen that a relatively low luminance value satisfies over a substantial angular range, but as the source becomes smaller than about 30 degrees, its luminance has to be increased quite sharply. However, it is when we get down to the really small sources that the source luminance has to escalate in order to provide the required illuminance, as shown in Figure 5.19.

It can be seen that when α = 180 degrees, $L_S = 100/\pi$, or approximately 31 cd/m². Reducing α to 90 degrees requires L_S to be doubled, but this is still a large source. When α comes down to 30 degrees, L_S has to be increased to 475 cd/m², and at 10 degrees it has to be over 4000 cd/m². However, it is when we get to a source subtending less than 10 degrees that the luminance value really climbs. A source subtending just 1.0 degree has to have a luminance of nearly half a million cd/m² to deliver just 100 lux.

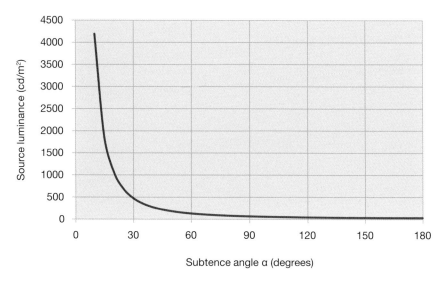

FIGURE 5.18   As the subtence of a large disc source is reduced, the source luminance required to maintain an illuminance value of 100 lux increases rapidly as subtence falls below 30 degrees.

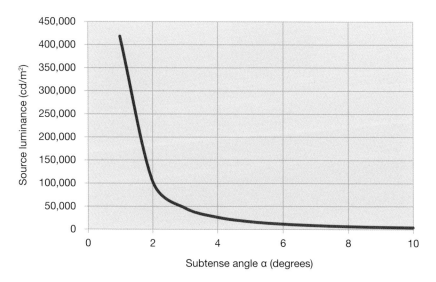

FIGURE 5.19   For small sources, the increase in luminance required to maintain 100 lux increases dramatically for subtence angles less than 3 degrees.

Imagine now that you want to deliver a given illuminance E_{tgt} onto a three-dimensional target, and you have selected a location for the luminaire at distance D. The required source luminous intensity $I_S = E_{tgt} \times D^2$ cd (for a two-dimensional target you will need to take account of the angle of incidence), so you scroll through the luminaire manufacturers' websites looking for a spotlight with suitable performance. While most manufacturers will give you intensity data, they are unlikely to give source luminance values, but clearly this will affect substantially the perceived 'sharpness', so you will need to check this for yourself. From the source dimensions, work out the luminous area A_S projected towards the object, and then the source luminance $L_S = I_S/A_S$ cd/m^2. This is your first step towards assessing the potential for 'sharpness'.

Highlight contrast potential (HCP)

Generally, smooth dielectric (non-electroconducting) materials have specular components of their total reflectance of around 4 per cent (although for electroconducting materials, such as polished metals, it can be much higher). Typically then, the luminance of the reflected highlight seen on a glossy surface $L_{hl} = 0.04\ L_S$, where L_S is the source luminance. The visibility of the highlight depends primarily on the luminance contrast of the highlight against the background on which it is seen.

The highlight contrast potential (HCP) is a measure of the extent to which a light source may provide a visible highlight. For this we ignore light that may be reflected from the surrounding environment (the highest possible highlight contrast will occur in a black environment where S is the only source of light) and consider a dielectric target surface *tgt* that has a reflectance ρ_{tgt} (which includes the 0.04 specular component) illuminated by source S, then the highlight luminance:

$$L_{hl} = 0.04 L_S$$

And the luminance of the target surface:

$$L_{tgt} = \frac{E_{tgt}\rho_{tgt}}{\pi}$$

Applying the disc source formula as previously,

$$E_{tgt} = \pi\frac{L_S}{2}(1 - cos\alpha)$$

So,

$$L_{tgt} = \frac{\pi L_S}{2}\frac{(1 - cos\alpha)\rho_{tgt}}{\pi}$$

$$= 0.5\ L_S(1 - cos\alpha)\rho_{tgt}$$

Then Highlight Contrast Potential:

$$HCP = \frac{L_{hl} - L_{tgt}}{L_{tgt}}$$

$$= \frac{0.04 - 0.5\rho_{tgt}(1 - cos\alpha)}{0.5\rho_{tgt}(1 - cos\alpha)}$$

$$= \frac{0.08}{\rho_{tgt}(1 - cos\alpha)} - 1$$

(5.6)

Note that although L_S does not appear in this formula, the source subtence angle is in there. If there are no other sources of light, then the only other factor determining HCP is target reflectance. In reality, other sources of light will be present and they will have the effect of reducing the highlight contrast, so that for a given light source, this is an expression for its maximum potential to provide highlight contrast. Figure 5.20 shows how the conspicuousness of highlights is dependent on low diffuse reflectance, such as the black glass sample in the comparison panel, as well as small angular size of the light source.

General lighting practice seeks to avoid specular reflections, identifying them as 'veiling reflections', but designers should distinguish between highlights and veiling reflections. When we considered the appearance of the comparison panel (Figure 5.17) in the thought exercise, the effect of the large source was to create a grey cast over the

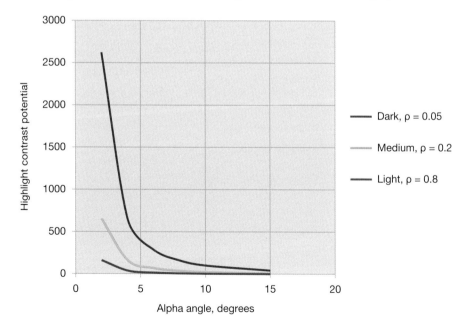

FIGURE 5.20 Highlight contrast potential HLC for three values of target reflectance, representing low, medium and high surface lightness, and a range of source angular subtence angles.

glossy black surface, reducing its blackness but giving no hint of its glossiness. This was a veiling reflection. However, when the source subtence was reduced, the specular reflection became a highlight pattern, seen in contrast against the undiminished blackness of the glass. If it had the effect of reducing the visibility of surface detail, this could easily be avoided by head movement, and meanwhile, the smooth, shiny surface of the glass would be given visual emphasis. The ability to create highlight patterns when and where required is an important skill in the lighting designer's toolkit. Again, mathematical analysis of a readily observed characteristic of lighting gives insight into its occurrence that is not intuitive.

That we have an expression for HCP does not mean that target values should be set, or that we have another factor to be calculated and measured. What matters is that we are able to identify the physical parameters on which HCP depends, and this enables designers to exercise control over the aspects of lighting that are influential. In the section entitled 'The three object lighting patterns' (page 66) it was noted how the appearance of some objects can be brought alive by highlight patterns, while others benefit from their complete absence. The usefulness of HCP lies in enabling design decisions to be guided by understanding of the conditions that govern the 'sharpness' of lighting.

The appearance of shadow patterns

Shadow patterns might seem to be the simplest of the three types of lighting patterns to come to terms with, but this is not so. While the perceived strength and direction of a shadow pattern relates to the VSR and the vector direction, its 'sharpness' relates to the HCP. In this way, the appearance of the shadow patterns within a space vary with both the overall impression of the 'flow' of light and the perceived 'sharpness' of the illumination.

Look once more at Figure 5.2, and note the role of 'sharp' shadow patterns, both those cast onto objects and those cast onto the background, in creating the appearance of depth and a sense of 'crispness' within the overall scene. As has been discussed, achieving these effects may support design objectives, as in Figure 5.4, or the situation may call for their avoidance, as in Figure 5.7. It is all a matter of being able to visualise the space and its objects in light, and being able to control lighting patterns to reveal, or to subdue or to emphasise surface attributes.

Figure 5.21 shows the formation of the penumbra, the extent of which is inversely related to the perceived 'sharpness' of a shadow pattern. Meanwhile, the apparent density of the umbra is determined by the VSR, and in this way we can see how the concepts of the three object lighting patterns – the shading, highlight and shadow patterns – are concepts that can readily be visualised and discussed with clients and other design professionals. On the other hand, the concepts of 'flow' and 'sharpness' of illumination provide means for describing illumination in terms of its potential to create object lighting patterns, and as such, they can enable members of a design team to build a shared understanding of three-dimensional light fields that fill spaces and influence appearances of everything within it. That both of these concepts – 'flow' and 'sharpness' – can be specified in terms of photometric concepts – vector/scalar ratio, vector direction, and highlight contrast potential – enables them to be described with confidence that they will be provided. The means for doing this are described in the next chapter.

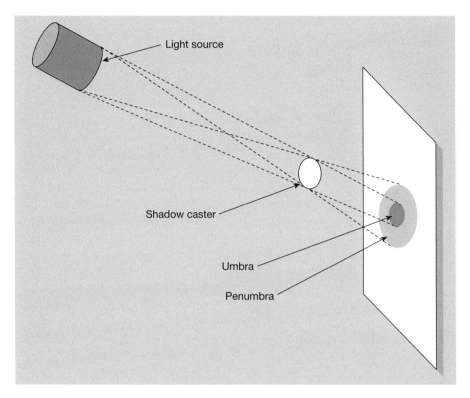

FIGURE 5.21 Light sources of smaller subtence angle produce less penumbra, increasing the 'sharpness' of the lighting. The perceived density of the umbra is determined by the strength of the 'flow' of light.

References

Cuttle, C. (1971). Lighting patterns and the flow of light. *Lighting Research and Technology*, 3(3): 171–189.

Cuttle, C., W.B. Valentine, J.A. Lynes and W. Burt (1967). Beyond the working plane. *Proceedings of the 16th Session of the CIE*. Washington DC, Paper P67–12.

Gershun, A.A. (1939). The light field. (Translation by Moon, P. and G. Timoshenko.) *Journal of Maths and Physics*, 18: 51–151.

Lam, W.M.C. (1977). *Perception and Lighting as Formgivers for Architecture*. New York: McGraw-Hill, Inc.

Lynes, J.A., W. Burt, G.K. Jackson and C. Cuttle (1966). The flow of light into buildings. *Transactions of the Illuminating Engineering Society (London)*, 31(3): 65–91.

Protzman, J.B. and K.W. Houser (2005). On the relationship between object modeling and the subjective response. *Leukos*, 2(1): 13–28.

Simons, R.H. and A.R. Bean (2001). *Lighting Engineering: Applied Calculations*. Oxford: Architectural Press.

Worthy, J.A. (1990). Lighting quality and light source size. *Journal of the Illuminating Engineering Society (New York)*, 19(2): 142–148.

6

DELIVERING THE LUMENS

Chapter summary

Throughout this book, the aim has been that a lighting designer should develop the skill to visualise the distribution of light within the volume of a space in terms of how it affects people's perceptions of both the space and the objects within it. These envisioned distributions of light comprise reflected light, while the distributions that the designer controls are the direct light to be provided by the lighting installation. Furthermore, they are, for the most part, three-dimensional variations of the light field, and the concept of cubic illumination is introduced to provide a basis for understanding them and enabling predictive calculations. Procedures are explained for specifying lamps and luminaires of correct performance, as well as controls to enable installations to respond to daylight availability. Measurement procedures are described for ensuring that design objectives have been achieved, and two Cubic Illumination spreadsheets are introduced that perform the calculations automatically.

Lighting calculations

Lighting calculations do not solve problems. Their purpose is to enable a designer to specify a layout of lamps, luminaires and control circuits with a reasonable level of confidence that it will create an envisioned appearance. No matter how well thought through the envisioned appearance might be, it will not be achieved by guesswork or 'hoping for the best'. Lamp wattages, luminaire spacings and beam spreads need to be correct for the distribution and balance of the lighting to look right.

Even so, some common sense needs to be applied. Photometric laboratories do, very properly, work to high levels of precision to specify the performances of lighting products, but while lighting designers need to have confidence in the reliability of the data that they are working with, precision in what they provide needs to be no better than differences that users (perhaps critical users) are likely to notice.

The aim has to be that a client who has had a lighting design proposal described in terms of perception-based objectives will be satisfied that their expectations have been met. Specifying and predicting performance in terms of lighting metrics, followed by checking the actual performance levels achieved, are necessary parts of the design process, but need not unduly concern clients.

Lighting design should not be thought of as a linear process, but nonetheless, this chapter follows a sequence that relates, quite sensibly, to a rational design procedure.

Mean room surface exitance, MRSE

Starting from how brightly lit, or dimly lit, the space is to appear, the designer decides upon a level of ambient illumination and specifies this in terms of mean room surface exitance, as explained in Chapter 2 and referring to Table 2.1. The general expression is:

$$MRSE = FRF / A\alpha \tag{6.1}$$

where FRF is first reflected flux:

$$FRF = \sum E_{s(d)} \cdot A_s \cdot \rho_s \tag{6.2}$$

and $A\alpha$ is the room absorption:

$$A\alpha = \sum A_s(1 - \rho_s) \tag{6.3}$$

where:

$E_{s(d)}$ = direct illuminance of surface s (lux)
A_s = area of surface s (m^2)
ρ_s = reflectance of surface s

Estimating the reflectance of a surface is not as simple as it might seem. Patterned surfaces are particularly difficult, but reasonably reliable measurements can be made by attaching an internally blackened cardboard tube to a light meter, as shown in Figure 6.1, and taking a reading of the surface in question, taking care to avoid specular reflections. Then, without moving the meter, slide a sheet of white paper over the surface and take a comparative reading. Good quality writing paper typically has a reflectance around 0.9. Alternatively, paint manufacturers often quote reflectance values for their products, and a paint colour swatch can be used to make matches to surface colours.

It is sometimes useful to be able to determine the equivalent reflectance of a cavity plane, ρ_{eq}, such as that of a luminaire plane, in which case the upper walls and the ceiling form the cavity. Start by calculating the ratio of the area of the cavity plane A_{cp} to the area of the cavity surfaces A_{cs}, and the average reflectance of surfaces within the cavity, ρ_{av}, then:

$$\rho_{eq} = \frac{\rho_{av}(A_{cp} / A_{cs})}{1 - \rho_{av}[1 - (A_{cp} / A_{cs})]} \tag{6.4}$$

FIGURE 6.1 Measuring surface reflectance, using an internally blackened cardboard tube fitted over an illuminance meter. Comparative readings are taken of the surface, avoiding specular reflections, and of a sheet of white paper.

When using formula 6.3 to calculate the room absorption value, $A\alpha$, it is often convenient to use A_{cp} and ρ_{eq} values. After that, the total first reflected flux required to provide the MRSE value is calculated:

$$FRF = MRSE \cdot A\alpha \tag{6.5}$$

This FRF value is the number of 'first bounce' lumens that has to be provided to achieve the design value of MRSE, and ways of accounting for this value are explained in 'Illumination hierarchy design' (page 32). It needs to be noted that room surface reflectance values are much more strongly influential in MRSE calculations than in conventional HWP calculations, and it is important that designers work with realistic values. The bad old practice of assuming room surface reflectance values is a recipe for disaster.

Illumination hierarchy and target illuminance values

After selecting the design value for the ambient illumination, the lighting designer decides upon the illumination hierarchy, which determines the distribution of illumination within the space. This is achieved by providing direct illumination selectively onto specific surfaces and objects, as demonstrated in Boxes 3.1 and 3.2, using the Illumination Hierarchy spreadsheet. The schedule of TAIR values is the first crucial statement of design objectives. The principal tool for devising this distribution is the classic *inverse square cosine law* (sometimes referred to as the 'point-to-point' formula), which is stated as:

$$E_P = \frac{I_S \cdot cos\theta}{D^2}$$

(6.6)

Where

E_P = illuminance at point of incidence P (lux)
I_S = luminous intensity due to light source S (candelas)
θ = angle of incidence
D = distance from source S to point P (metres)

This statement of the law is often accompanied by a diagram of the sort shown in Figure 6.2 in which the whole issue of providing direct illumination is reduced to two dimensions and, by default, it often happens that the plane of incidence is assumed to be the horizontal working plane.

Once we become concerned with providing illumination onto planes that people actually look at, we are likely to find ourselves dealing with situations that are far more like Figure 6.3. Here point P is on a vertical surface which may be of any orientation, and illuminated by a directional light source S. The location of S relative to P is determined by dimensions X, Y and Z (which may be positive or negative according to direction), and then, depending on circumstance, it can be convenient to think of Y as being in the 'eye' direction, so that X is 'a-cross' and measures positive to the right and negative to the left, while on the vertical axis, Z measures positive up and negative down. It can be handy to keep this picture in mind as it can avoid a lot of confusion when it comes to analysing measured data.

The performance of the light source S is indicated by its distribution of luminous intensity, I_S, specified in candelas (cd), and often this can be simplified into two essential items of performance data. These are the intensity value on the beam axis, which for historical reasons is still often referred to as the centre beam candle power (CBCP), and the beam angle, B, for which the beam edge is defined by the angle at which intensity drops to 50 per cent of the CBCP value. For example, if CBCP = 3000cd and B = 12°, then at 6° to each side of the beam axis, intensity I_S = 1500cd. Any light emitted outside the beam should be regarded as 'spill', and blocked by louvres or baffles.

First we will consider how to use these data to calculate the illuminance E_P at point P. Then we take note that, providing the beam is conical, it forms an elliptical pattern on the surface, with minor and major axes q' and q". These too we need to be able to predict, particularly as we often need to use several light sources to build up a pattern of overlapping ellipses to provide coverage over a target surface. Also, it needs to be kept in mind that, following the procedures described in the foregoing chapters, the purpose may

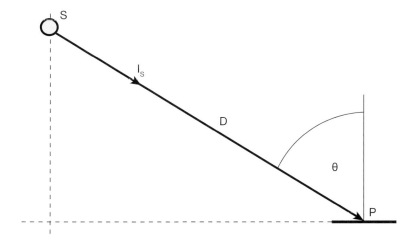

FIGURE 6.2 Application of the point-to-point formula, $E_P = I_S \cos\theta/D^2$, for determining the illuminance at point P on a horizontal plane. I_S is the beam centre luminous intensity.

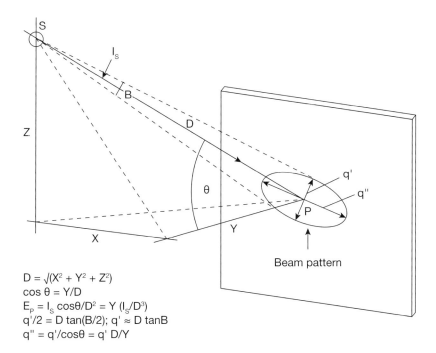

$D = \sqrt{(X^2 + Y^2 + Z^2)}$
$\cos\theta = Y/D$
$E_P = I_S \cos\theta/D^2 = Y\,(I_S/D^3)$
$q'/2 = D\tan(B/2); \ q' \approx D\tan B$
$q'' = q'/\cos\theta = q'\,D/Y$

FIGURE 6.3 Determining the illuminance at point P on a vertical plane, and the beam pattern formed on the plane. B is the beam angle, which defines the cone over which luminous intensity equals more than 50% of I_S, the CBCP value.

be to provide the direct illumination required to provide the target/ambient illuminance ratios (TAIRs) determined for the illumination hierarchy. Keep in mind that this means that we need to start off knowing the illuminance that is required, and the aim is to determine the luminous intensity to be provided. As we look though suppliers' data for suitable luminaires, we check the suitability of potential luminaires by noting their CBCP and B values.

Application of the inverse square law to the situation shown in Figure 6.3 calls for some careful examination of the situation. Pythagoras' theorem tells us that the distance D of P from S is given by $D = \sqrt{(X^2 + Y^2 + Z^2)}$, but what seems a little more tricky in this three-dimensional situation is finding the cosine of the angle of incidence, θ. This is the angle that the beam axis forms with the y axis, which is the normal to the surface at P, so that $\cos\theta = Y/D$. Look back to Formula 6.6, and it can be seen that we can rewrite the formula for calculating the illuminance at P as:

$$E_P = Y \frac{I}{D^3}$$

(6.7)

Take good note of this 'D to the 3' expression. By eliminating cosθ we have greatly simplified the 'point-to-point' calculations, and we will make use of this formula. It may be rearranged to give the required source intensity to achieve E_P:

$$I_S = E_P \cdot D^3 / Y$$

(6.8)

Now we turn our attention to the elliptical beam pattern formed on the surface. This pattern becomes crucial when we are selectively illuminating a chosen surface from some distance. According to the shape of the surface, it may be necessary to build up coverage of overlapping ellipses using several light sources.

Referring again to Figure 6.3, it can be seen that:

$$q' / 2 = D. \, tan(B / 2)$$

and unless B is large, in which case the beam flux method described in Section 6.7 is likely to be more suitable, this expression may be approximated to:

$$q' = D. \, tanB$$

(6.9)

Note also that cosθ = Y/D, so that:

$$q'' = q' / \cos\theta = q'.D / Y$$

(6.10)

These handy expressions, which enable illumination to be provided onto vertical surfaces evenly and with minimal spill, are summarised on Figure 6.3. Inclined surfaces can also be dealt with by keeping in mind that Y is the dimension on the surface normal at P. For the mathematically agile, an even more versatile approach employing vector algebra is available (Cuttle, 2008).

As the perimeter of the beam pattern ellipse is defined by the contour where luminous intensity drops to half the beam axis value, even coverage of a surface is achieved by butting ellipses up edge to edge. It is reasonable to assume that the average illuminance within an individual ellipse is 75 per cent of the calculated E_p value.

The D/r correction

There is a lingering concern. The *inverse square cosine law* is referred to as the 'point-to-point' formula for a good reason. It is based on the concept of a point source illuminating a point on a surface, and of course, point sources are hypothetical as they have no area. It may be shown that error will be not more than 1 per cent if the distance D is at least five times the maximum dimension of the luminaire d, and on this basis it is generally recommended that use of 'point-to-point' formulae is restricted to situations where $D > 5d$. In practice, many situations may occur where D will be less than 5d, particularly where there is a need to get in close with the lighting or large, diffusing light sources are being used. For these situations various 'area source' formulae have been published, but they tend to be cumbersome. A more simple solution is to stay with the prediction formulae based on the inverse square cosine law and to apply the *D/r correction*.

Figure 6.4 shows a point P illuminated alternatively by two light sources, both at distance D and normal to the surface at P. S1 is a hypothetical point source, and S2 is a diffusing disc source of radius r and normal to the direction of P. For S1, the illuminance at P is:

$$E_{S1} = I_{S1} / D^2$$

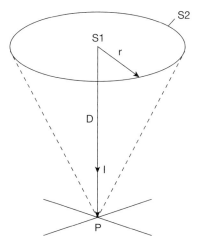

FIGURE 6.4 The point P is illuminated by two alternative sources, S1 being a point source and S2 a luminous disc of radius r. Both sources are at distance D.

For S2, we apply the disc source formula (Simons and Bean, 2001):

$$E_{S2} = M_{S2} \frac{r^2}{D^2 + r^2}$$

where M_{S2} is the exitance of source S2.

For a diffusing source, the luminous intensity normal to the surface equals the luminous flux output divided by π, so that:

$$I_{S2} = \frac{M_{S2}\pi r^2}{\pi} = M_{S2}r^2$$

So:

$$E_{S2} = \frac{I_{S2}}{r^2} \times \frac{r^2}{D^2 + r^2} = \frac{I_{S2}}{D^2 + r^2}$$

If we assume that $I_{S1} = I_{S2}$, and we apply the more simple E_{S1} expression to calculate the illuminance due to an area source, the illuminance value will be overestimated. This could be overcome by applying a (D/r) correction:

$$C_{(D/r)} = \frac{E_{S2}}{E_{S1}} = \frac{I}{D^2 + r^2} \times \frac{D^2}{I}$$

$$= \frac{D^2}{D^2 + r^2} \tag{6.11}$$

Note that D is the distance S to P, and r is the radius, or half the maximum dimension, of the light source normal to the direction of P.

The value of $C_{(D/r)}$ can be read from Figure 6.5 and applied directly to calculations using Formulae 6.6 or 6.7. It may be noted that the value of D/r needs to reduce to a low value before the correction makes much difference, in fact, the source radius has to approach the distance before the error becomes really significant. Added to that, it may be noted that Formula 6.11 assumes that the light source is a luminous disc of diameter 2r that is normal to the direction of P, and this defines the 'worst case' situation. If a linear source is used instead of a disc source, the $C_{(D/r)}$ correction will overestimate the illuminance reduction by about one-third. The reality is that when we assume a point source we are tending to overestimate illuminance, and when we assume a disc source, we are tending to underestimate. Unless the source is large in relation to the distance, sensible judgment will suffice.

In this way, Formula 6.11 enables simple 'point-to-point' expressions to be applied for a wide range of practical lighting situations, and the $C_{(D/r)}$ correction may be applied with reasonable confidence wherever the aim is to illuminate a two-dimensional surface with a source that is other than small in relation to its distance from the surface. Practical examples might include selected room surfaces, or pictures displayed on them, or freestanding panels, as well as any surfaces for which target/ambient illuminance ratios, TAIRs, have been specified as part of the illumination hierarchy planning.

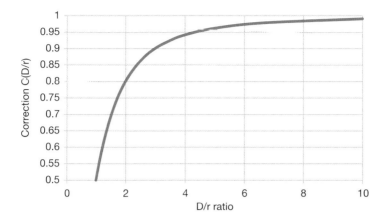

FIGURE 6.5   The correction factor $C_{(D/r)}$ to be applied to point source illumination formulae to allow for the ratio of distance D to source radius r.

It may be noted that the classic 'point-to-point' formula (Formula 6.6) could be restated in a generally applicable form:

$$E_P = \frac{I_S \cdot cos\theta}{D^2 + r^2}$$

$$(6.12)$$

We will now move on to consider three-dimensional applications of these formulae, where examples are given that deal with both two-dimensional surfaces and three-dimensional objects.

Cubic illumination

The principle of cubic illumination (Cuttle, 1997) is illustrated in Figure 6.6. As has been explained in Chapter 5, the illumination distribution about a point in three-dimensional space, however irregular, may be represented as the sum of two simple distributions. One of these is defined by a vector solid that accounts for the entire asymmetry of the illumination distribution about a point, while the other is a symmetric solid that is, as its name suggests, entirely symmetric about the point. To analyse an illumination distribution into these components, we calculate (or measure) the illuminance values on the six faces of a small cube centred at the point, orientated so that its facets are normal to the x, y and z axes, as shown in Figure 6.6. The x and y axes lie in the horizontal plane and the z axis is vertical, and the six facet illuminance values are designated $E_{(x+)}$, $E_{(x-)}$, $E_{(y+)}$, $E_{(y-)}$, $E_{(z+)}$ and $E_{(z-)}$. If these conventions are adhered to, the procedure for dealing with six illuminances at a point becomes surprisingly painless.

  Distances of source S from P on the axes are indicated by X, Y, and Z dimensions which may be positive or negative according to direction, as shown in Figure 6.7. The location of the cube is X = Y = Z = 0, which would be recorded as (0,0,0), and if we refer back to Figure 6.3, it can be seen that if we were to replace the two-dimensional surface shown there with the three-dimensional cube, the location of the light source S would be indicated by (X-, Y-, Z+) dimensions.

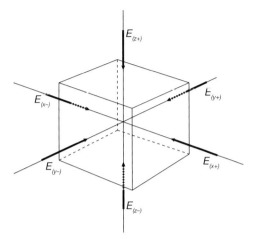

FIGURE 6.6 The Cubic Illumination concept. The spatial distribution of illumination at a point is characterised by six illuminance values on the facets of a cube centred at the point, with the facets aligned normal to the x, y, and z axes. From these six values, the illumination vector magnitude and direction can be defined, and the scalar illuminance can be estimated.

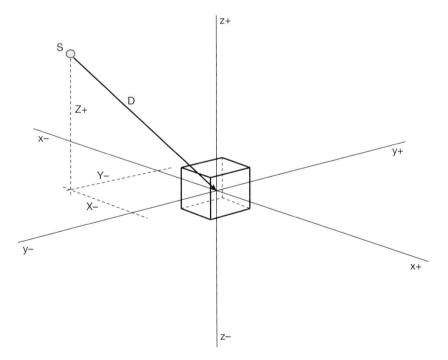

FIGURE 6.7 The location of source S relative to a three-dimensional object is defined in terms of X, Y, and Z dimensions, which may be positive or negative according to direction.

Looking back to Formula 6.7, we can define the cubic illuminance values as:

$$E_{(x)} = X \frac{I}{D^3} \tag{6.13}$$

$$E_{(y)} = Y \frac{I}{D^3} \tag{6.14}$$

$$E_{(z)} = Z \frac{I}{D^3} \tag{6.15}$$

According to the signs of the X, Y, and Z dimensions, the illuminance values may be positive or negative, so that if $E_{(x)}$ has a positive value, that illuminance is incident on the (x+) facet of the cube, and if negative, it is incident on the (x–) facet. It follows that positive and negative $E_{(x)}$ values have to be summed separately, and negative values do not cancel positive ones.

Consider a 50 watt halogen reflector lamp, such as the MR16 EXT, which we will identify as S1, and this source is aimed so that its peak beam candlepower (I_S = 9150 candelas) is directed towards P. The location of S1 relative to P is defined by the dimensions X = −1.9m, Y = −2.7m, and Z = 3.2m. Then:

$$D = \sqrt{((-1.9)^2 + (-2.7)^2 + (3.2)^2)} = 4.6m$$

and

$$I_S/D^3 = 9150/(4.6)^3 = 94.1$$

Then from formulae (6.13–6.15):

$$E_{(x)} = X (I/D^3) = -1.9 \times 94.1 = -179 \text{ lux}$$
$$E_{(y)} = Y (I/D^3) = -2.7 \times 94.1 = -254 \text{ lux}$$
$$E_{(z)} = Z (I/D^3) = 3.2 \times 94.1 = 301 \text{ lux}$$

Yes, it really is as simple as that: no angles, no cosines and three illuminance values for the price of one. However, it is necessary to keep an eye on those signs. Note that $E_{(x)}$ = −179 lux is simply another way of writing $E_{(x-)}$ = 179 lux. As we add the contributions from different sources on each facet of the cube, we add separately the sums of $E_{(x+)}$ values and $E_{(x-)}$ values, as they are the illuminances on opposite sides of the cube.

This example shows the underlying process for determining the six direct cubic illuminance values, but for practical calculations we again utilise the facilities of a spreadsheet. Box 6.1 shows the output of the Cubic Illumination spreadsheet, and as previously, the only data to be entered by the user are those in red, as all other data are calculated automatically. In the box, source S1 from the foregoing example is shown, and three more sources have been added. Rather than have a separate spreadsheet for two-dimensional surfaces, it is more simple to use this spreadsheet and to keep in mind that, following the view direction convention shown in Figure 6.3, the $E_{(y-)}$ value gives the surface illuminance.

BOX 6.1

CUBIC ILLUMINATION SPREADSHEET
140121

| Project: | | Box 6.1 |
| MRSE | 150 lm/m² | |

Distances S-P

Source	Is (cd)	X+	X-	Y+	Y-	Z+	Z-
S1	9150	0	1.9	0	2.7	3.2	
S2	6200	0	4.1	1.9		2.8	
S3	5800	3.2			1.7		0.8
S4	7220	0	2.6		0.9	3.4	
S5		1					
S6		1					

Source	D	I/D³	E(x+)	E(x–)	E(y+)	E(y–)	E(z+)	E(z–)
S1	4.5	94.1	0	178.8	0	254.1	301.2	0
S2	5.3	41.2	0	169.2	78.4	0	115.5	0
S3	3.7	113.5	363.2	0	0	192.9	0	90.8
S4	4.3	86.2	0	224.3	0	77.6	293.3	0
S5	1	0	0	0	0	0	0	0
S6	1	0	0	0	0	0	0	0
	Total E³ values		513.2	722.4	228.4	674.7	860.1	240.8

Vector components		Symmetric components				
Evr(x)	–209.2	Esym(x)	513.2		Evr	791.6
Evr(y)	–446.3	Esym(y)	228.4		Esym	327.4
Evr(z)	619.3	Esym(z)	240.8		Esr	525.3
					Esr(d)	375.3

Vector/scalar ratio		Unit vector components		Vector direction	
Evr/Esr	1.51	e(x)	-0.264	α 51°	
		e(y)	-0.564		
		e(z)	0.782		

Notes
Enter data only in cells shown in red.

Is = luminous intensity of S in direction of P.

MRSE is the design level of ambient illumination within the space.

Check Distances S-P: either a '+' or a '–' dimension; never both.

For a typical outdoor application it would be necessary to consider only the direct illuminance values on the six faces of the cube, but otherwise, the effect of ambient illumination needs to be included. As shown in Box 6.1, the user specifies the MRSE value to be provided within the space by the entire lighting installation. Each of the six cubic illuminance values will be the sum of direct and indirect values, and the MRSE value is added to each direct cubic illuminance value to represent the effect of indirect light. This assumes that the contribution of indirect light is uniform for all six facets, and while this avoids the tedious process of making a precise evaluation of the indirect illuminance onto each facet of the cube, some caution needs to be observed. For a situation where the distribution of reflected flux is likely to be distinctly asymmetric, such as where an object is located close to a dark wall surface, this simplification could lead to a misleading outcome, and users need to be alert for this. Even so, the assumption is not unreasonable. In an indoor space where the proportion of indirect illumination is low, it will have little visible effect and so it would be a waste of time to evaluate its spatial distribution. Where the proportion of indirect light is high, it is likely to be highly diffused by multiple reflections from light-coloured room surfaces so that its contribution to the visible effect will be to soften the directional effect of the direct light rather than to impart a distinct directional effect. The user should be alert for situations where indirect light could be both dominant and directional, and for a more rigorous treatment of indirect illuminance, see Simons and Bean (2001).

The reason for predicting, or measuring, the cubic illuminance values is to enable vector analysis of the illumination solid, and the Cubic Illumination spreadsheet performs the analysis to produce Box 6.1 by applying the formulae given in the previous section. The great benefit of using spreadsheets is not simply that they automate the calculations, but that they enable the user to explore alternative options, and the reader is strongly encouraged to access the spreadsheet and to experience how this is done. It is simple to change a light source, or to move it from one location to another, and instantly the effects on the vector/scalar ratio (VSR) and the vector direction are given, so that the user can envisage how an arrangement of luminaires will influence the 'flow' of light, and how this might affect the perception of a selected three-dimensional object.

Providing an illumination hierarchy

An illumination hierarchy expresses a lighting designer's concept for the overall appearance of a lit space. It specifies the ambient illumination level as a mean room surface exitance (MRSE) value, and it expresses how the distribution of direct flux from the luminaires will affect the relative appearances of specified targets in terms of a distribution of target/ambient illuminance ratios (TAIR) values.

The effect of ambient illumination upon the impression of the brightness or dimness of illumination within a space is at least as much determined by the MRSE level in adjacent spaces as by the actual level within the space, and both Tables 2.1 and 2.2 need to be considered for making a design decision. As described in Chapters 2 and 3, Table 2.2. is used also for making decisions about TAIR values, and it can be seen that for target illumination to be even noticeable, a TAIR value of at least 1.5 is necessary, with higher levels needed to achieve distinct or strong effects. Emphatic differences can be difficult to achieve, as unless very high target illuminance values are to be used, they call for distinctly low levels of MRSE.

A schedule of direct illuminance levels to be provided onto each selected target can be generated from the MRSE and TAIR values:

$$E_{tgt(d)} = MRSE \ (TAIR_{tgt} - 1) \tag{6.16}$$

The sum of individual target FRF values gives the total first reflected flux due to direct illumination of all target surfaces:

$$FRF_{ts} = \sum E_{tgt(d)} \cdot A_{tgt} \cdot \rho_{tgt} \tag{6.17}$$

For two-dimensional targets, $E_{tgt(d)}$ is the average direct illuminance, and for three-dimensional targets, the best guide is the direct component of the scalar illuminance, where $E_{sr(d)} = E_{sr} - MRSE$. This value can be read from the Cubic Illumination spreadsheet (Box 6.1).

The level of first reflected flux (FRF) that is required to provide the design value of ambient illumination, specified in terms of MRSE, comprises the sum of components due to direct light reflected from target surfaces (FRF$_{ts}$) and from room surfaces (FRF$_{rs}$):

$$FRF = FRF_{ts} + FRF_{rs} \tag{6.18}$$

Refer back to Boxes 3.1 and 3.2 and note the distinction that was made between first reflected flux due to illumination directed onto target surfaces with the aim of establishing an illumination hierarchy, and first reflected flux that was then required to bring the ambient illumination up to the MRSE design value. While targets need significant levels of selective illumination directed onto them in order to achieve appreciable differences of appearances, for providing illumination onto other surfaces to bring up the MRSE level, the aim should be to keep the $E_{tgt(d)}$/MRSE well below 3.0, and preferably below 1.5 (although this can be difficult), so that the flux directed onto these surfaces will not noticeably detract from the illumination hierarchy.

From Formula 6.16, it follows that FRF$_{rs}$ = FRF – FRF$_{ts}$, and to provide this both efficiently and with low $E_{tgt(d)}$/MRSE will need one or more large, high-reflectance room surfaces to receive direct flux. The ceiling is often the obvious choice, but other options should be sought. A series of illuminated white ceilings can have a bland overall effect.

Before looking further at calculational procedures, it should be acknowledged that a very effective way to explore design options for providing FRF$_{rs}$ is to use a proprietary lighting design software package such as AGI32 or DIALUX. The trick is to set all surface reflectance values to zero, so the program gives you direct surface illuminance values. These packages usually give serious attention to working plane (or floor) uniformity and provide precise-looking illuminance contours, while giving only average illuminance values for walls and ceiling, so it pays to give attention to how the appearance of these surfaces may be affected by luminaire spacing. However, used in this way, these packages can provide a useful design facility.

Lighting techniques such as cove lighting onto ceilings, wallwashing and recessed lighting onto floor planes are widely used for providing room surface illumination, but do not overlook opportunities for suspended (and visible) pendant luminaires, or incorporating lighting into furniture or handrails. Whatever lighting technique is employed, selection of suitable luminaires involves careful examination of the angular relationships between the source locations and the receiving surfaces. Where multiple sources are to be used, choose sources with beam angles that are smaller than the subtence angle of the receiving surface, but large enough to provide full coverage from overlapping beams. The number of luminaires required is:

$$n = FRF_{rs} / (F_B \cdot \rho_S)$$
(6.19)

where Γ_B is the 'beam flux', or the quantity of lumens within the beam(s).

Manufacturer's data for lumen outputs of directional luminaires have to be examined with care. The only lumens that count are those within the beam, as those outside the beam are 'spill' and need to be blocked or shielded. For luminaires with conical beams (i.e., not shaped beams as in wallwashers) it is generally recognised that beam width is measured to the direction in which the luminous intensity falls to 50 per cent of the maximum value (Figure 6.3), and usually the quoted angle is whole angle from edge to edge of the beam, although sometimes it is the half-beam angle, measured from the beam axis to the edge. For this text, the whole beam angle is given the symbol B, and the half-beam angle is b.

Because it is not always clear whether 'lumen output' data refer to the entire output of the luminaire or just the beam lumens, the most reliable way of determining the value is to work from data for the luminous intensity distribution, given in candelas. The beam flux, in lumens, is given by:

$$F_B = 1.5I_{max} \cdot \pi(1 - \cos b)LD$$
(6.20)

here:

I_{max} = maximum beam luminous intensity, or CBCP, in candelas
b = half beam angle
LD = lumen depreciation factor

Consider the MR16 EXN halogen lamp, which has a beam angle of 36° and a CBCP of 1800cd. Allowing for a lumen depreciation of 0.8, $F_B = 1.5 \times 1800 \times \pi(1 - \cos(18°)) \times 0.8 = 332$ lm. It should not escape notice that the luminous efficacy for beam lumens for this lamp is just 6.6 lm/W, and that is not allowing for transformer losses. It is clear that even with the precision focussing that these lamps achieve, a significant proportion of the filament lumens do not find their way into the beam. This 'spill' light is not only a concern from the point of efficiency, but also for achieving a controlled distribution of light. Reflector lamps should always be housed in luminaires that are shrouded or have baffles or louvres to intercept light spill. This becomes particularly important where spill onto surfaces adjacent to the luminaires could produce very bright unwanted lighting patterns.

It is in this way that a layout of luminaires is developed that will deliver the required quantity of lumens onto each selected room surface. The designer's aim is to devise a flux distribution that will provide the first reflected flux for the required ambient illumination, together with the range of TAIR values that will achieve the envisaged illumination hierarchy.

Daylight illumination

Lighting designers may, from time to time, become involved in fenestration design for special applications, such as the windows for an observation tower or a picture gallery skylight, but regrettably, it is much more usual practice (in this author's experience) that by the time a project is introduced to a lighting designer, others have determined the layout of windows, clerestories and skylights, as well as the type of glazing, sunshading and blinds to be installed. In case some readers should find themselves confronted with demands for advice that differ from my experience, it may be noted that there is no shortage of books on daylighting practice written for architects. However, this section is based on the assumption that the lighting designer's task is restricted to devising electric lighting installations that may from time to time need to respond to significant presence of daylight.

The principal means for assessing the performance of a daylighting installation has for many years been the *daylight factor*, and despite a fair amount of recent activity aimed at improving the modelling of outdoor daylight availability, the daylight factor continues to be concerned with provision of illumination onto indoor horizontal working planes (HWPs). In this section, a quite different approach is proposed. Every indoor space needs to have an electric lighting installation. Where there is significant daylight admission, the appearance of that space and its contents will be affected at different times and in different ways, and a lighting designer needs to give thought to how the electric lighting installation is to respond to the presence of daylight. This is to take account of both achieving what may be perceived to be an appropriate balance of illumination at all times, while at the same time gaining energy savings from reduced use of electric lighting.

Opportunities for either of these objectives vary hugely, and some elaborate evaluation systems have been proposed. Taking a simple approach, fenestration systems can be broadly categorised as side windows, clerestories, or skylights – or some combinations of those types. Their impacts upon lighting design may be assessed in terms of the contributions they make towards provision of ambient illumination, target illumination, view-out and energy efficiency (Figure 6.8).

Skylights can provide very effectively for ambient illumination, as well as providing for HWP illumination. As has been discussed, ambient illumination, indicated by the MRSE level, is concerned with how inter-reflected light influences the appearance of surrounding room surfaces, whereas the daylight factor is concerned with enabling effective performance of visual tasks located on desktops or work benches. Skylights that are designed so that sloped glazing is orientated in the polar direction (north-facing in northern hemisphere; south-facing in southern hemisphere) can provide fairly consistent, diffused, ambient illumination over much of the year, and this should be taken into

	Side windows	Clerestories	Skylights
Ambient illumination	★	★★	★★★
Target illumination	★★	★	
View-out	★★★	★	
Energy efficiency	★	★★	★★★

★★★	Good prospects
★★	Moderate prospects
★	Limited prospects

FIGURE 6.8 Assessment of likely prospects for various roles for fenestration in buildings.

account in developing an electric lighting installation to provide room surface illumination out of normal daylight hours. The daytime and night time illumination distributions may be quite different, requiring careful thought about the transitions between these two conditions. Progressive photoelectrical control is likely to be the option of choice, and for large area, single-storey buildings, the prospects for doing this effectively and attractively by daylight are good (Figure 6.8). By comparison, successful provision of ambient illumination by clerestory windows is restricted to spaces having fairly high height/width proportions, and more limited still, are side windows. This is not to imply that they are necessarily ineffective, but rather that their use for providing useful ambient illumination is more restricted, particularly where they occur only in one wall. It is common experience that windows in one wall can provide all the illumination required for much of the time in spaces of domestic scale, but that becomes uncertain in spaces where the room width is more than double the height of the window head.

Effective target illumination favours electric lighting as the reliable means for setting up an illumination hierarchy, but nonetheless, nothing can compare with the impact created when side windows enable an object, such as a sculpture, to be positioned to 'catch the light' as discussed in Chapter 5. It is, perhaps, the obviously transitory nature of the experience that adds to its appeal. To design fenestration specifically for the purpose of providing target illumination raises the issue of how to integrate that illumination with electric lighting to take over when daylight is inadequate. Where the circumstances are seen to demand it, careful attention to achieving effective target illumination by daylight can be very rewarding, but otherwise it needs to be recognised that the ever-changing nature of daylight makes it a difficult source to use where the appearance of a specific target forms an important component of the designer's overall concept.

The suitability of side windows for providing view-out might seem to be too obvious to warrant discussion, but in fact, misdirected thinking on this issue is so common that it really does need some careful attention. Most surveys of building occupant satisfaction have been conducted on office workers, and again and again, they report daylight as being a highly rated option, and this has been translated into standards demanding that specified minimum daylight factor values are provided over some specified percentage of the HWP. The well-known fact that, in open plan offices, desks that are located close to windows are regarded as prime locations, despite their much lower ratings on thermal comfort indices, is widely accepted as confirmation of this preference. However, rethinking the basis of this preference in terms of provision of view is likely to lead to distinctly different design options. Side windows designed for view-out combined with reasonably high levels of thermal comfort would be quite different from windows designed to maximise daylight admission. In particular, they would be likely to incorporate sunshading devices, fixed or adjustable, specifically designed for the orientation of the window, and which would intercept sunlight with minimal obstruction of view-out.

So far, little attention has been given to energy efficiency, although this topic is discussed in the final chapter. It should not be a matter of surprise that prospects for energy efficiency are shown in Figure 6.8 to be in step with daylight provision of ambient illumination. This is because daylighting systems that have good prospects for ambient illumination are likely to also have good prospects for photoelectric control that will balance electric light use against daylight availability. The essential difference from common practice is how photosensors are located and commissioned. Sensors need to respond to levels of inter-reflected light within the space, and so they need to be shielded from direct light from both the daylighting and the electric lighting systems. For example, in a space with side windows, a good location for a sensor is mounted vertically on the wall above the window head, and shielded from direct light from the electric lighting installation so that it is exposed to reflected light within the room, but not to direct light. This is quite different from conventional practice, which is directed by the notion that the purpose for admitting daylight into buildings is to provide working plane illumination. The role that daylight can fulfil best of all is providing ambient illumination.

It may be noted that where the foregoing procedures have led to an electric lighting installation that provides, out of daylight hours, an effective illumination hierarchy through a combination of target and room surface illumination, the prospect exists for effective lighting control by dimming just the room surface illumination. In this way, an effective daytime balance of ambient illumination with a maintained illumination hierarchy may be achieved with worthwhile energy savings.

Checking delivery: measuring the lumens

The on-site measurable illumination quantities that are integral to this perception-based approach to lighting design are:

*   mean room surface exitance, MRSE
*   target/ambient illuminance ratio, TAIR
*   vector/scalar ratio, VSR, and vector direction.

While highlight contrast potential (HCP) has also been introduced as a relevant metric, its usefulness is for making comparisons at the design stage, rather than as a metric to be checked on site. Also, at the time of writing, there are no generally available meters for checking metrics relating to the spectral distributions of illumination, but this may be about to change. CCD-based spectrometers have recently become reasonably affordable, and this could lead to the availability of portable instruments capable of making on-site measurements of many of the visible and non-visible factors discussed in Chapter 4.

It is an essential part of acting as a professional lighting designer that the performance of every installation is checked against the predicted performance, regardless of whether the client has shown interest in the data. There never will be a perfect match, but knowing the nature and extent of the departures is how a designer gains feeling for exercising control over perceived aspects of illumination.

Measuring MRSE

While MRSE is reasonably straightforward to calculate, it is not obvious how to obtain a reliable measure of its quantity. Conventional light meters have been developed to give measurements of lumen density incident on a surface, without regard for the direction from which the light is incident. MRSE is not related to any particular surface of incidence, and it discriminates according to the origin of arriving light. It takes account only of indirect light, and disregards light arriving directly from light sources, and this creates a difficulty for measurement.

The purpose of MRSE is to provide us with a useful measure of ambient illumination, and that means that we need to make a measurement that relates to light arriving at the eye, rather than light incident on things that people might choose to look at. Figure 6.9 shows a simple approach. Choose a position and direction of view that, while it takes in much of the space, avoids light from windows, table lights and so forth, and then hold a luxmeter up to the eye and shield it from any luminaires before taking a measurement. Depending on the size of the space, repeat this for other positions to obtain an average value. Making measurements in this way can provide a reasonable indication of the extent to which a predicted MRSE value has been realised, and this is valuable information for the designer.

Proposals have been made for more rigorous procedures for MRSE measurement (Cuttle, 2013). This approach involves using high dynamic range imaging to produce a

FIGURE 6.9 A simple way of making an approximate measurement of MRSE using a conventional light meter. Expose the meter to a wide view of the space avoiding, as far as possible, windows and other light sources, and shield direct light from any overhead luminaires.

widc-field image of a space defined in terms of luminance. Light sources could then be identified and excluded, so that the remaining field of view would represent the total inter-reflected illumination. It is to be hoped that such a system will one day become available, particularly as it could enable not only measurement of MRSE, but also of discomfort glare.

Measuring TAIR

The next step in evaluation will be to check TAIR values. Once again, the designer will have explained the illumination hierarchy in terms of perceived difference, and will have planned the luminaire layout to achieve specified TAIR values. Checking by measurement devclops confidence in relating appearance to metrics, as well as application of metrics for determining required luminaire performance.

For a two-dimensional target, TAIR = E_{tgt}/MRSE, which is quite straightforward, but measuring E_{tgt} for three-dimensional targets can pose difficulties. If practical, it is usually best to move the target to one side and to measure the cubic illumination at the spot, using the procedure described in the following paragraphs, from which the direct component of scalar illuminance is determined by use of the Vector Measurement spreadsheet, which is described in the following paragraphs. Otherwise, measurements corresponding to the cubic illumination axes may be taken over the object's surface, but it should be noted that if a particular direction of view is significant in the overall appearance of that object within the space, then a single measurement normal to that direction might provide for a better indicator of how well the TAIR value relates to the illumination hierarchy.

Measuring VSR

It might seem that the most straightforward way to measure the six cubic illuminance values would be to mount a small cube at the measurement point and take successive readings on the cube's facets, but in fact, this procedure is cumbersome and tedious, particularly when it comes to taking the measurement on the downward facing facet. Various cubic illumination meters incorporating six photocells have been developed, such as the one shown in Figure 6.10, but it is worth taking note of a simple procedure that makes use of just one photocell mounted on a photographic tripod (Cuttle, 2014).

Envisage the cube tilted, as indicated in Figure 6.11, so that a long corner-to-corner diagonal of the cube is vertical, and three facets of the cube face upwards and three downwards. The familiar x, y, z spatial axes are unchanged, but now the axes of the cube are designated u,v,w. Figure 6.12 shows a vertical section through the tilted cube on the y axis, where BC is one external edge of the cube, AB is a facet diagonal and AC is the vertical long diagonal. The ratios of the triangle sides BC, AB and AC are 1, $\sqrt{2}$, and $\sqrt{3}$, and the angle a = a′ = $\sin^{-1} 1/\sqrt{3}$ = 35.3°. This is the angle by which the u, v and w axes are tilted relative to the horizontal plane, and as shown in Figure 6.11, the u axis is assumed to lie in the same vertical plane as the y axis.

To make the cubic illumination measurements, a right-angle bracket is constructed to support the photocell vertically on the head of a photographic tripod, as shown in Figure 6.13. It helps to have a tripod with a spirit level to ensure verticality and with the horizontal and vertical movements scaled in degrees. The measurement procedure is then straightforward. Set the photocell tilt to $+35°$ as shown in Figure 6.14, and rotating the horizontal movement of the tripod, read $E_{(u+)}$ at $0°$, $E_{(v+)}$ at $120°$ and $E_{(w+)}$ at $240°$. Reset the photocell tilt to $-35°$, and read $E_{(u-)}$ at $180°$, $E_{(v-)}$ at $300°$ and $E_{(w-)}$ at $60°$.

FIGURE 6.10   A six-photocell cubic illumination meter. This instrument is self-levelling and is connected to a laptop computer that automatically analyses the data. Photographed at the Lighting Research Center, Rensselaer Polytechnic Institute, Troy, New York.

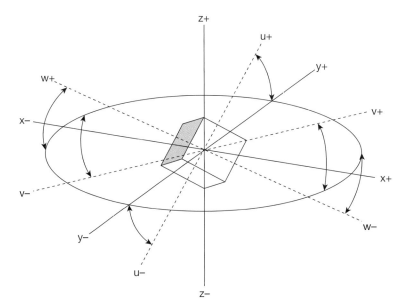

FIGURE 6.11 The measurement cube is tilted so that a long axis is coincident with the z axis, and three facets face upwards and three downwards. The facets are normal to the u, v, and w orthogonal axes.

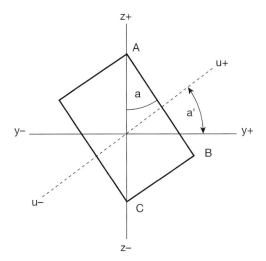

FIGURE 6.12 A vertical section through the tilted cube on the u axis, which lies in the same vertical plane as the y axis, against which it is tilted through the angle a.

FIGURE 6.13 A photocell head mounted on a right–angle bracket, onto a photographic tripod.

FIGURE 6.14 The photocell tilted to +35° relative to the horizontal plane, and ready for measuring the three-dimensional illumination distribution.

Box 6.2 shows the output of the Vector Measurement Spreadsheet. The only data to be entered by the user are the six measured values, and from these a range of derived data relating to the spatial illumination distribution is given based on formulae given in Chapter 5. While the illumination vector magnitude is derived directly from the measured data, the output data for vector direction are converted from u, v, w axes to the more familiar x, y, z axes, using the following formulae:

$$e_{(x)} = 0.707(e_{(v)} - e_{(w)})$$

(6.21)

$$e_{(y)} = 0.816e_{(u)} - 0.408(e_{(v)} + e_{(w)})$$

(6.22)

$$e_{(z)} = 0.577(e_{(u)} + e_{(v)} + e_{(w)})$$

(6.23)

While there are other lighting quantities that are relevant to the design process, such as correlated colour temperature and the highlight contrast, application of these concepts need not involve calculations and so confirmation by measurement is not usual practice. Nonetheless, when designers are verifying that all is according to expectations, it is necessary that every aspect of interaction between the lighting installation and the space and its contents must come under scrutiny.

BOX 6.2

CUBIC ILLUMINATION MEASUREMENT (u,v,w)

140121

Project	Box 6.2

Illuminance data input

E(u+)	109	E(u-)	311
E(v+)	365	E(v-)	305
E(w+)	342	E(w-)	70

Illuminance components

E(u)	-202	~E(u)	109
E(v)	60	~E(v)	305
E(w)	272	~E(w)	70

Vector and scalar data

E	344	~E	161
Esr	247	E/Esr	1.39

Horizontal and cylindrical data

Ewp	236		
Ecl	268	Ecl/Ewp	1.13

Vector direction (unit vector)

e(u)	−0.587	e(x)	−0.436
e(v)	0.174	e(y)	−0.873
e(w)	0.791	e(z)	0.218
e(u,v,w)	1	e(x,y,z)	0.999

Vector direction (altitude and azimuth angles)

e(x,y)	0.975	alpha	12.7
e'(y)	−0.895	phi	−154.7

Notes

Input data shown in red only. All the rest are generated automatically.

alpha (vector altitude) may be +ive or -ive re horizontal

If phi (vector azimuth) = +ive then anticlockwise re y- axis; else clockwise

References

Cuttle, C. (1997). Cubic illumination. *Lighting Research & Technology,* 29(1), 1–14.

——(2008). *Lighting by Design: Second edition.* Oxford: Architectural Press.

——(2013). A new direction for general lighting practice. *Lighting Research & Technology,* 45(1): 22–39.

——(2014). A practical approach to cubic Illumination measurement. *Lighting Research & Technology,* 46(1): 31–34.

Simons, R.H. and A.R. Bean (2001). *Lighting Engineering: Applied Calculations.* Oxford: Architectural Press.

7

DESIGNING FOR PERCEPTION-BASED LIGHTING CONCEPTS

Chapter summary

The development of a lighting design proposal involves bringing together the variety of perception-based lighting concepts into a balance that relates to the design objectives specific to the location. It requires the ability to envision a space and its contents in light, and seen in this way, the volume of the design space ceases to be a void, and instead is perceived as a three-dimensional light field creating interactions with room surfaces and the objects within the space. It is from this envisioned concept that the designer develops understanding of the required characteristics of the light field, leading to the layout of luminaires and light sources, together with strategies for their control. A flowchart linking the lighting concepts to metrics and procedures is introduced. Where the procedures involve calculations, their purpose is seen to be to increase the designer's level of confidence that the design objectives, stated in terms of perception-based concepts, will be achieved. The design outcome is a comprehensive lighting equipment specification.

Achieving perception-based lighting concepts

We now turn our attention to the task of applying the range of perception-based lighting concepts that has been discussed in the foregoing chapters. Each and every project is a fresh challenge that calls for understanding of the various roles that the space and its contents are planned to serve, backed up by the designer's creative imagination directed towards influencing people's perceptions of the space, its setting, and its contents through lighting.

Seen in this context, the lighting concepts provide a framework for ordering thinking about lighting's potential for influencing people's visual experiences of their surroundings. These range from overall impressions of brightness or dimness of spaces encountered in a sequence of entering and passing through a building; the ways in which the spectrum of light may arouse or subdue both visual and non-visual responses; through to ordered distributions of illumination that differentiate activities within spaces and which relate to the visual significance of objects; and on to the lighting patterns that reveal the form, texture, glossiness, or translucency of individual objects. Within the volume of a space, illumination may, at one extreme, be softly diffused, revealing everything without emphasis; and at the other extreme, be selective and sharply directional, differentiating surfaces and objects with clarity. As part of the same visualisation, lighting may on one hand be perceived as being without apparent source, or on the other hand, sources of light may be clearly expressed components of the scene. This is the gamut of variety (or at least a good part of it!) that a creative designer may bring to bear upon a project, and the perception-based lighting concepts provide means for both ordering creative thinking and exercising control.

While design is not to be reduced to a step-by-step procedure, the flowchart shown in Figure 7.1 presents a rational ordering of the lighting concepts and gives an overall guide to this section.

Ambient illumination

Is the first impression to be of a brightly lit space, or a dimly lit space, or something in between? This issue has been discussed in the sections in Chapter 2 entitled 'The MRSE conecpt' and 'Applying the ambient illumination concept in design', and it requires careful thought. A person visiting the space will inevitably experience it within a sequence, arriving from outdoors or from another indoor space, before moving on. It may be their destination, or a space that they will experience in passing. Perhaps the design aim is to arouse attention, or alternatively, to provide a place for rest. The possibilities are limitless, as are the roles that lighting may play, but throughout, the connection between the overall sense of brightness and the first impression is strong. Tables 2.1 and 2.2 together provide a simple introduction to ambient illumination, but it is up to the designer to develop sensitivity to the relationships that may arise.

While MRSE (mean room surface exitance) may be an unfamiliar concept, it is surprisingly easy and rewarding to come to terms with. The notions of visualising light within the volume of a space rather than incident on surfaces, and of thinking in terms of light at the eye, so that we achieve our aims through providing reflected light, and direct light is simply a means to achieving that end, lead naturally to effective lighting applications. The Ambient Illumination spreadsheet is a useful tool for the first stage of linking a vision to a luminaire layout.

Illumination colour appearance

Apart from the brightness or dimness of ambient illumination, its colour appearance can significantly affect the appearance of a space. Illumination that is basically 'white' may nonetheless have a distinct tint, and the acceptability, or even the attractiveness, of that tint, can be strongly affected by context and people's expectations.

As has been explained, the generally accepted practice is to specify the tint of 'white' illumination by CCT (correlated colour temperature) where low values (CCT < 3200K) are associated with yellowish–white light and 'warm' colour appearance, and high values

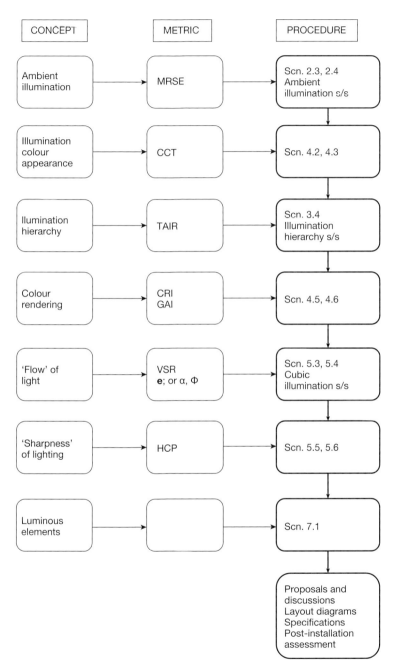

FIGURE 7.1 A lighting design flowchart. Follow through each row from concept, to metric, to procedure. The sequence of concepts is proposed as being logical, but may be adapted to suit circumstances. The aim is to develop proposals for discussion, which would lead to the design proposal. Post-installation assessment and measurement should also be included as part of the design process.

(CCT > 5000K) with bluish–white light and 'cool' colour appearance. At present, this is the choice that the lighting industry offers, but research findings have been noted (page 46) which indicate that light source chromaticities departing from the black-body locus may offer preferred colour appearance alternatives.

Illumination hierarchy

Situations occur where totally diffused illumination that reveals without emphasis can be highly effective, but more usually some ordering of illumination distribution is called for. There may be various reasons for this. The aim may be to distinguish between zones within a space; it may be to increase the visibility of selected detail; or it may be to draw attention to objects of visual significance. The ability to envision a structured distribution of illumination is a defining skill of a lighting designer, but it needs to be understood that while the envisioned effect is a distribution of reflected flux, it is achieved by providing a distribution of direct flux onto selected targets that will generate that distribution. This ability to separate in the mind the applied distribution of direct flux and the resulting distribution of reflected flux is crucial. It is an acquired skill that evolves from careful observation of how appearance is affected by the balance of direct flux applied to targets, and of diffusely-reflected ambient illumination.

The notion of an illumination hierarchy, by which the lighting designer's concept of emphasis forms the basis of a structured illumination distribution, is set out in terms of TAIR (target/ambient illumination ratio). The Illumination Hierarchy spreadsheet is a useful tool for seeing through this stage of the procedure.

Colour rendering

CRI (colour rendering index) is the readily available metric, and its limitations have been discussed at some length. CRI serves the needs of specifiers, but designers need more. The GAI (gamut area index) adds an indication of colourfulness to that of fidelity, but too often the values on this scale are unavailable. Really useful information, such as CMV (colour-mismatch vector) data, is unlikely to be available, so that designers need to develop through directed observation, as described in the section 'Source spectrum and human responses' in Chapter 4, the experience to be able to select light sources with colour rendering properties that really suit particular applications.

The 'flow' of light

The directional properties of a light field that generate shading patterns through interactions with three-dimensional objects provide a dynamic quality to the appearance of a space. This aspect of lighting is particularly associated with spaces lit by side windows, and where daylight creates strong 'flow' of light effects, careful consideration needs to be given to how the electric lighting is to respond to the varying shading patterns. Distinct shading patterns on individual objects are easily produced by spotlights, but the 'flow' of light concept refers to a lighting effect that creates a coherent sense of illumination distribution within a space.

The VSR (vector/scalar ratio) relates to the perceived strength of the 'flow', and the direction of 'flow' may be indicated by the unit vector **e**, or by the vector altitude and azimuth angles.

The 'sharpness' of lighting

The potential for lighting to generate highlight patterns on glossy-surfaced three-dimensional objects is indicated by the HCP (highlight contrast potential), which also relates to the perceived 'sharpness' of shadow patterns and the overall appearance of the 'crispness' of lighting.

Luminous elements

This is the only one of the concepts listed in Figure 7.1 that has not been discussed in the text, but it is in fact the easiest of all the concepts to come to terms with. Often it would be true to say that, for lighting designers, the perfect luminaire would be invisible. As it is, designers often strive to eliminate as far as possible any visible intrusion of luminaires into the scenes that they create. Luminaires are recessed into ceilings, tucked above shelves or cornices, or built-in under furniture or handrails. They are, for the most part, regarded as necessary but unwelcome intrusions into the scene.

There are, however, times when the luminaires become features of the design concept. There can be all sorts of reasons for this, but a recurring one is that the space is bland and featureless, and would benefit from the presence of self-luminous, eye-catching objects that add 'sparkle' and interest to the scene. There are no metrics for assessing the perceived effect nor are there procedural steps for incorporating these elements into the design, but when the decision is made that luminous elements are to be part of the scene, it is as well to keep in mind the well-worn adage, "One man's sparkle is another man's glare".

The design product

The spreadsheets that have been used to generate the Boxes shown alongside the text facilitate the translation from envisioned effects to luminaire performance not only by performing the calculations, but by providing the designer with almost unlimited opportunity to explore alternative options. Designers are encouraged to use them as models to develop spreadsheets that serve their own fields of lighting practice. Commercially available 'lighting design' software packages generally fail to address the issues that concern a creative designer.

While most people think of a lighting designer's output being the illumination that users will experience, the realities of life should cause the designer to take a different attitude. It is the specification document, listing lamps, luminaires, circuits and controls, that determines whether or not his or her vision of a space in light will be achieved, and for this reason, the specification should be regarded as the design product. It has been stated above that the ability to envision is the essential design skill, but the ability to translate that vision into a specification document that will not be compromised runs it a close second. Never lose sight of the fact that when the specification goes out to tender, the contractor who will get the job will be the one that puts in the lowest price.

Defining illumination adequacy

While this 'perception-based approach' to lighting design is proposed as being appropriate for indoor lighting applications ranging from simple, everyday activities to complex, large-scale projects, it cannot be denied that there will always be some situations for which it would be quite sensible to provide uniform illumination over the time-honoured horizontal working plane, *wp*, which extends wall-to-wall and may be coincident with the floor plane, or elevated above it.

This type of lighting practice is sometimes referred to as 'lumen dumping', and the conventions adopted by lumen dumpers for planning their lighting installations include treating every space as a rectangular room measuring $L \times W$, with the lighting installation comprising a regular grid of luminaires located on the luminaire plane, *lp*, which may be coincident with the ceiling or below it, and with only the wall height H between *lp* and *wp* being counted as wall area *w*. All of these dimensions are inter-related by the room index, where $RI = L.W/H(L+W)$. (North American practice uses the room cavity ratio, where $RCR = 5H(L+W)/L.W = 5/RI$.)

Clearly this approach contrasts with that adopted by the rest of this book, so let us now imagine what would be the implications for lumen dumpers if the designated lighting standard were to be based on perceived adequacy of illumination, PAI, being prescribed minimum level of ambient illumination, specified in terms of mean room surface exitance, MRSE.

The defining expression states that MRSE equals the first reflected flux FRF divided by the room absorption $A\alpha$, so that:

$$MRSE = \frac{FRF}{A\alpha}$$

and:

$$FRF = MRSE \times A\alpha$$

Room absorption is the sum of products of room surfaces (work plane, luminaire plane, and walls) and their absorptance values:

$$A\alpha = A_{wp}(1 - \rho_{wp}) + A_{lp}(1 - \rho_{lp}) + A_w(1 - \rho_w)$$

It is common in such situations for room surface finishes to be undefined, and for 'typical' surface reflectances to be assumed. Providing that assurances are given that 'light' finishes will be used, the following surfaces' reflectances may be assumed as typical:

$$\rho_{wp} = 0.25; \ \rho_{lp} = 0.75; \ \rho_w = 0.5$$

Applying these reflectance values to the above expression gives:

$$A\alpha = L.W + H(L + W)$$

So:

$$FRF = MRSE[L.W + H(L + W)] \tag{7.1}$$

The first step for determining a lighting layout is to use Formula 7.1 to calculate the first reflected flux, after which the next task is to devise a distribution of direct flux from the lighting installation that will provide the required level of FRF, and this presents the lumen dumper with a novel quandary. There is no stipulated illumination distribution. At one extreme, s/he could direct all of the flux onto the work plane, but that might create the dreaded "cave effect". At the other extreme, all of the flux could be directed upwards into the cavity above the luminaire plane, and while that would be a very efficient way of providing the FRF, it would distract attention away from the work plane.

The concept of illumination hierarchy is all about providing controlled distributions of illumination, and for the lumen dumper, the solution would be to nominate the work plane as the target and to work towards a suitable target/ambient illumination ratio, TAIR.

Target illuminance is the sum of direct and indirect components, so that if we assume luminaires that direct all, or at least almost all, of the downward flux onto the work plane:

$$TAIR = \frac{E_{wp(d)} + MRSE}{MRSE}$$

$$= \frac{E_{wp(d)}}{MRSE} + 1 \tag{7.2}$$

From Formula 7.1:

$$TAIR = \frac{E_{wp(d)}[L.W + H(L + W)]}{FRF_{wp} + FRF_{lp}} + 1$$

$$= \frac{L.W + H(L + W)}{0.25L.W + UFFR.0.75L.W} + 1$$

where $UFFR$ = upper flux fraction ratio

$$TAIR = \frac{1 + \dfrac{1}{RI}}{0.25 + 0.75UFFR} + 1$$

Then:

$$UFFR = \frac{1 + \dfrac{1}{RI}}{0.75(TAIR - 1)} - 0.33 \tag{7.3}$$

In this way, both TAIR and UFFR are readily predictable for target work planes. If it is decided to use fully recessed luminaires, or any other type of luminaire for which UFFR = 0, then TAIR values can be read from Table 7.1. It can be seen that high values are unavoidable, particularly for low *RI* values.

These high TAIR values can be avoided by use of luminaires that have some upward light component. Figure 7.2 shows how UFFR values relate to TAIR, and this may be

TABLE 7.1 Values of target/ambient illuminance ratio, TAIR, against room index where the horizontal working plane, HWP, is the target surface and all direct flux is incident on the HWP. Light surface reflectances are assumed

RI	*TAIR*
1	9
2	7
3	6.3
4	6
5	5.8

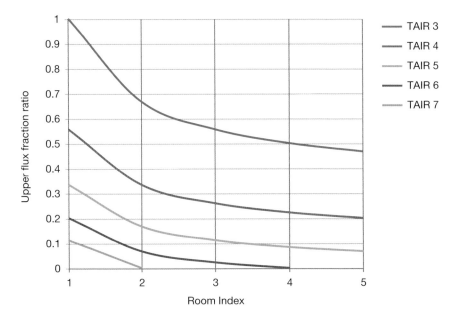

FIGURE 7.2   TAIR values for the horizontal working plane, when it is the target. Except for at low values, room index has only slight effect, but the upper flux fraction ratio is strongly influential.

seen as a simple version of a more comprehensive study reported by Lynes (1974). Jay (2002) has commented that a *BZ3* lighting installation with a 10 per cent upward light component provides a satisfactory appearance in a wide range of workplace applications, and Figure 7.2 shows this to relate typically to a TAIR value around 5 except at low *RI* values. To this I would add my own observation that it needs a TAIR value of at least 3 to impart a distinct difference of appearance to a target, and for a level much less than 2, the difference is unlikely to be noticeable.

The difference between this situation and current general lighting practice is that only the *amount* of light, as it influences assessment of illumination adequacy, is specified, and the distribution of that light is undefined. This means that for anyone to plan a lighting installation, some thought has to be given to the question; What is the purpose of the lighting? Perhaps a grid of luminaires providing uniform work plane illuminance is appropriate, but perhaps not. MRSE specifications may apply to many locations other than workplaces – in fact, the only exceptions would be locations where distinctly dim lighting may be a legitimate design objective. Generally it should be assumed that providing for PAI (perceived adequacy of illumination) does matter, and at the same time, that there needs to be scope for specific targets to be selected so that an illumination hierarchy can be drawn up in terms of TAIR values. It is in this way that an illumination distribution can be created that meets the specific requirements of a space without being compromised by the need to comply with a lighting standard that prescribes uniformity.

The important role of room surface reflectance values

It's time for another thought experiment. Suppose that you are designing a setting in which a white marble sculpture is to be displayed, and you want to achieve a stunning effect. You want the sculpture to stand out from its background so strikingly that it appears to glow. You want the highest possible target luminance contrast. Peter Jay has examined the condition of *maximum attainable contrast* (Jay, 1971) for which every lumen provided is incident on the target, and the background is illuminated only by light reflected from the target.

To simplify the situation, we will assume all surfaces to be diffusing reflectors so we can define maximum attainable contrast in terms of exitance (M) values for a target, *tgt*, seen against a background, *bg*:

$$C_{max} = \frac{M_{tgt} - M_{bg}}{M_{bg}}$$

(7.4)

In any enclosed space, the total room surface area, A_{rs}, is the sum of the areas of the enclosing surfaces and any objects contained within the space. If we direct all of the light from the luminaires onto a target area A_{tgt}, then the remainder of the surface area, which forms the background to the target, is A_{bg}, so that $A_{rs} = A_{tgt} + A_{bg}$. As the background receives only indirect illumination, the contrast for this condition will be the maximum attainable contrast, C_{max}. Target and background illuminances and reflectances are E_{tgt}, E_{bg}, ρ_{tgt} and ρ_{bg} respectively.

The target is completely enclosed in a space of exitance M_{bg}, and so the indirect component of its average illuminance will be equal to M_{bg}. The direct component of the target illuminance is therefore $E_{tgt} - M_{bg}$, and the total luminous flux from the luminaires is $A_t(E_t - M_b)$. We apply the conservation of energy principle to state that this flux must equal the rate of absorption by both the target and background areas, so that:

$$A_{tgt}(E_{tgt} - M_{bg}) = A_{tgt}E_{tgt}(1 - \rho_{tgt}) + A_{bg}E_{bg}(1 - \rho_{bg})$$

So:

$$A_{tgt}E_{tgt} - A_{tgt}M_{bg} - A_{tgt}E_{tgt} + A_{tgt}M_{tgt} = A_{bg}E_{bg}(1 - \rho_{tgt})$$

$$A_{tgt}(M_{tgt} - M_{bg}) = A_{bg}E_{bg}(1 - \rho_{bg})$$

Divide through by M_{bg}, noting Formula 7.4 and that $M_{bg} = E_{bg}\,r_{bg}$:

$$\frac{M_{tgt} - M_{bg}}{M_{bg}} = \frac{A_{bg}}{A_{tgt}} \times \frac{1 - \rho_{bg}}{\rho_{bg}} = C_{max}$$

(7.5)

This is Jay's formula for maximum attainable contrast (Jay, 1971). It shows that C_{max} is the product of two factors, one being the ratio of the surface areas, A_{bg}/A_{tgt}, and the other factor, $(1-\rho_{bg})/\rho_{bg}$, being dependent only on the background reflectance. Now think back to the white marble statue. These two factors tell us that to maximise the contrast, we need to put the statue into a space that is large in relation to the statue, and with low surface reflectance. There is nothing surprising about that, until we notice that there is no mention of target reflectance. If we were to replace the white marble statue with a black one, all the exitance values would be reduced proportionately, but the contrast would be unchanged.

Let's look at this formula a bit more carefully. The target reflectance has dropped out, and $(1-\rho)/\rho$ term is the background absorptance/reflectance ratio, α/ρ, and as shown in Figure 2.9, the inverse of this ratio, ρ/α, describes the influence of reflectance upon ambient illumination. Both of these ratios are plotted in Figure 7.3, where it can be seen that they mirror each other. This figure breaks down into three zones. Where the value of ρ is less than 0.3, room surface exitance will be substantially lower than direct illuminance. Here we have the potential to achieve high target/background contrasts, even where the target area is not much smaller than the background area. Moving to the other side of the chart, where ρ is greater than 0.7, room surface exitance exceeds direct illuminance by some margin, and while this will give an enhanced sense of overall brightness, reasonably high contrasts can be achieved only with targets that are much smaller than their surroundings. In the mid-zone, where ρ values are in the range 0.3 to 0.7, room surface exitance values will be fairly similar to direct illuminance values. This equal balance of direct and diffuse illumination components gives scope for providing noticeable (but not distinct) illumination differences while avoiding strong contrasts. It is also a prescription for practical room surface reflectance values, and guides for good

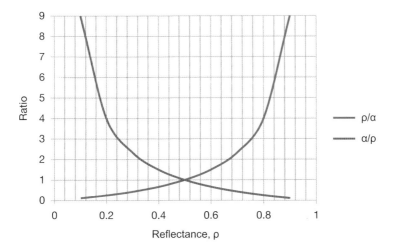

FIGURE 7.3 The influence of room surface reflection properties. For every surface, $\rho = 1-\alpha$, where ρ is reflectance and α is absorptance. From Formula 2.1 it can be seen that MRSE is proportional to ρ/α, and from Formula 7.3, maximum attainable contrast is proportional to α/ρ. Where overall room surface reflectance, ρ, is either more than 0.7 or less than 0.3, it's effect upon appearance will be pronounced.

lighting practice invariably recommend reflectances within this range. It may be looked upon as the safe range, in which there is some limited scope for emphasis, but providing sufficient light is put into the space, everything will appear adequately lit. However, this should not inhibit a creative designer. The important thing is for the designer to have developed, through observation of the impact that lighting can have on the appearance of lit spaces, the confidence to step outside the restrictions of recommended practice.

Jay's study extended beyond a target object surrounded by a background, to examine the limitations for contrast when the target is part of the space itself. Examples might be a demonstration area in a teaching space, or a dance floor in a restaurant. It must not be lost sight of that the formula is based on the assumption that 100 per cent of the provided luminous flux is incident on the target, so that ambient illumination outside the target area is due only to reflected flux. It is, after all, a formula for *maximum attainable* contrast, and so unlikely to be achieved in practice. However, it may be noted that as the target becomes a larger part of the total surface area, so it becomes realistic to assume that spill light onto the background is more likely to be significant, which has the disadvantage of reducing actual target contrasts, and the advantage of reducing the need to supplement the target lighting to provide for safe movement.

Final remarks

The perception-based lighting design approach proposed in this book leaves untouched some aspects of lighting that have traditionally been cornerstones of lighting policy. In particular, the topics of lighting for productivity in workplaces and efficient use of energy for lighting have been barely mentioned, and so we will close by looking at how these two aspects interact with this perception-based approach.

Lighting for productivity in workplaces

We live in an era in which if things need to be seen, they are designed to be seen. Examples of this surround us. Carbon copies were first replaced by photocopies, and then by laser printed materials, before paper-based materials in turn gave way to screen-based displays, originally CRT screens, which in turn have been replaced by high-definition, full-colour LED displays. At least, that is what has happened where material has to be read by a human being. Where the process of reading has been taken over by machines, such as the bar-code readers at supermarket checkouts, the visual task has not simply been eased, but has actually been eliminated, and similar examples can be found in many industrial workplaces.

This revolution in the role of vision has not been accompanied by any serious revaluation of the provision of illumination. Lighting standards and recommended practice documents specify illuminance values for visual tasks, and for anyone who cares to read the cited literature, these are claimed to be based on measured values of the luminance contrast and angular size of the critical detail at the eye. The reality is that while the specified illuminance has climbed during the previous half century, visual task difficulty has eroded or vanished. What has not changed is the notion that providing for illumination adequacy involves lighting the HWP (horizontal working plane) to a specified level, and because this is the basis of lighting standards, it applies to all manner of indoor applications. Every space from a waiting room to a precision machine shop is assessed by someone holding an illuminance meter at around waist height, and wandering around to ensure that at no point does the measured value drop below the specified one.

There are a few exceptions. Some visual tasks cannot be redesigned, and notable examples are surgery, for obvious reasons, and quality control inspection, where the aim is to detect even very slight defects in manufactured products. The common feature of these applications is that they call for specialised solutions that are quite separate from the general lighting. Consider, for example, that you have undertaken a project to light a dentist's premises. You think through the progression of a patient arriving at the entrance, advancing to the reception, and moving through to the waiting room before being called into the surgery. At every stage you have different ideas about the appearance that you want to create, and how you will use lighting to achieve it. However, once the patient is tilted back in the dentist's chair, and the dentist needs a few thousand lux on the patient's back molars, a completely different form of lighting takes over, and the way that that is provided is none of your concern. A luminaire that incorporates a high level of technical expertise is brought into use, but it is a component of the dentist's equipment and does not form part of the lighting installation.

It may be said that, generally, in an indoor space where there is an activity that involves the need for visibility, the surfaces associated with that activity should be designated as target surfaces and incorporated into the illumination hierarchy scheme. Examples would include art galleries, retail stores, industrial assembly lines, and the tellers' counters in banking premises. For activities that are particularly visually demanding, which include the already cited examples of surgery and quality control, specialised lighting solutions that are designed not merely to deliver lumens, but to enhance the visibility of the critical detail, are to be applied. Wherever people are to spend long working periods, whether visually demanding or not, provision for perceived adequacy of illumination requires attention. If high levels of target illumination are to be applied, then keeping TAIR down to modest values will have the effect of ensuring appropriately high levels of MRSE.

Efficient use of energy for lighting

It goes without saying that energy efficient lighting must make use of high luminous efficacy light sources in optically efficient luminaires. Beyond this, the lighting needs to provide for PAI (perceived adequacy of illumination), no more and no less, at all times that the space is occupied. This may involve a control system that can dim the electric lighting to take account of daylight availability, and that will switch it off when the space is unoccupied. The important way in which this differs from good current lighting practice is that it relates to PAI, which means that the lighting sensor is installed so that it responds to MRSE, and not to HWP illuminance. The thinking behind this is that the space should always appear adequately lit without ever being lit to excess, and that instead of the designer working to keep inside a lighting power density limit (W/m^2), the aim would be a genuinely low energy installation, measured in $kWh/m^2.yr$.

While this scheme seems reasonably straightforward, it could lead to the illumination hierarchy being compromised. Overall dimming to allow for changing levels of daylight would inevitably change the balance of the lighting, particularly in situations where the designer has put together an installation that provides different TAIR values, and involves different types of light sources focussed onto different targets. In such circumstances, it may be an effective policy to maintain the selective target lighting, and to dim only lighting that is provided to boost MRSE, particularly that which washes light over room surfaces close to the source of daylight.

So the question arises, would changing from conventional practice of specifying illumination requirements in terms of minimum HWP illuminance, to basing it upon satisfying PAI, lead to lower energy consumption? The first thing to make clear is that this perception-based approach is not proposed as means for reducing lighting levels. The basic requirement is that a space should appear adequately lit, taking account of the viewer's likely expectations. Conventional practice can, on occasion, lead to the 'cave effect', a dismal appearance brought about by the misguided pursuit of high efficiency. To restate the illumination standards in MRSE values should have the effect of preventing this unfortunate outcome. However, it has to be understood that the prescribed lux (or lm/m^2) values would need to be substantially lower than the current HWP values, not because less light is to be provided, but because of the different way in which the metric evaluates the level of illumination provision.

So if the aim is to come up with the ultimate energy efficient solution that will satisfy the PAI criterion by providing a prescribed MRSE level, what would be the outstanding features of such an installation? The most obvious difference would be the appearance of the space itself. Every surface within such a space would be white or chromium plated! To experience the space would be like stepping into an integrating sphere. Every lumen emitted within the volume of the space would be guaranteed longevity. It would undergo a prolonged life of multiple reflections before eventually being absorbed by the room surfaces. To get an idea of why this would be so, take a look at Figure 7.3. The ρ/α would be so high that it would take the emission of only a few lumens to build up a high lumen density within the space. Of course high efficacy light sources and high efficiency luminaires would be applied, so that only a very low power density would be required to meet any reasonable MRSE value.

Look now at the α/ρ function in Figure 7.3, and it can be seen that as potential for MRSE rockets upwards with increasing room surface reflectance, potential for contrast gets ever lower. We are looking at an environment in which everything is visible, but nothing has distinct visibility. There is no illumination difference, whether a planned illumination hierarchy or an arbitrary outcome of source and distance, and there is no 'flow', and there is no 'sharpness'.

Compared with this outcome, it can be seen that lighting that relates to space, objects, and particularly to people, comes at a cost. Seen in this way, current notions of good lighting practice do, in fact, represent one particular type of energy efficiency compromise. To pursue perception-based lighting concepts is to bring different factors into the equation. Luminaire performance is still there, but the room and its contents are to be seen as the secondary luminaire, whose role is to deliver luminous flux to the viewer. The role of the primary luminaires (the lighting hardware) is to energise the secondary luminaire. This process should be engineered for effectiveness and efficiency.

References

Jay, P.A. (1971). Lighting and visual perception. *Lighting Research & Technology*, 3: 133–146.
——(2002). Subjective criteria for lighting design. *Lighting Research and Technology*, 34: 87–99.
Lynes J.A. (1974). Illuminance ratios as a constraint on utilance. *Lighting Research and Technology*, 6: 172–174.

APPENDIX

Abbreviations used in the text

α	Absorptance, or vector altitude angle
φ	Vector azimuth angle
ρ	Reflectance
A, Aα	Area, room absorption (m^2)
CAM	Colour appearance model
CBCP	Centre beam candle power (cd)
CCT	Correlated colour temperature (K)
CGA	Colour gamut area
CQS	Colour quality scale
CMV	Colour mismatch vector
CRI	Colour rendering index
D, D/r	Distance (m), distance/radius correction
E, $E_{s(d)}$	Illuminance, direct illuminance on surface s (lx)
E, **E**$_{(x)}$	Vector illuminance, vector illuminance component on x axis (lx)
e, **e**$_{(x)}$	Unit vector, unit vector component on x axis
~E, ~E$_{(x)}$	Mean symmetric illuminance, symmetric illuminance on x axis (lx)
FRF	First reflected flux (lm)
HCP	Highlight contrast potential
HWP	Horizontal working plane
M_S	Exitance from surface s (lm/m^2)
MRSE	Mean room surface exitance (lm/m^2)
PAI	Perceived adequacy of illumination (MRSE)
RI	Room index
S/P	Scotopic/photopic ratio
TAIR	Target/ambient illuminance ratio
TCS	Test colour sample
VSR	Vector/scalar ratio

INDEX